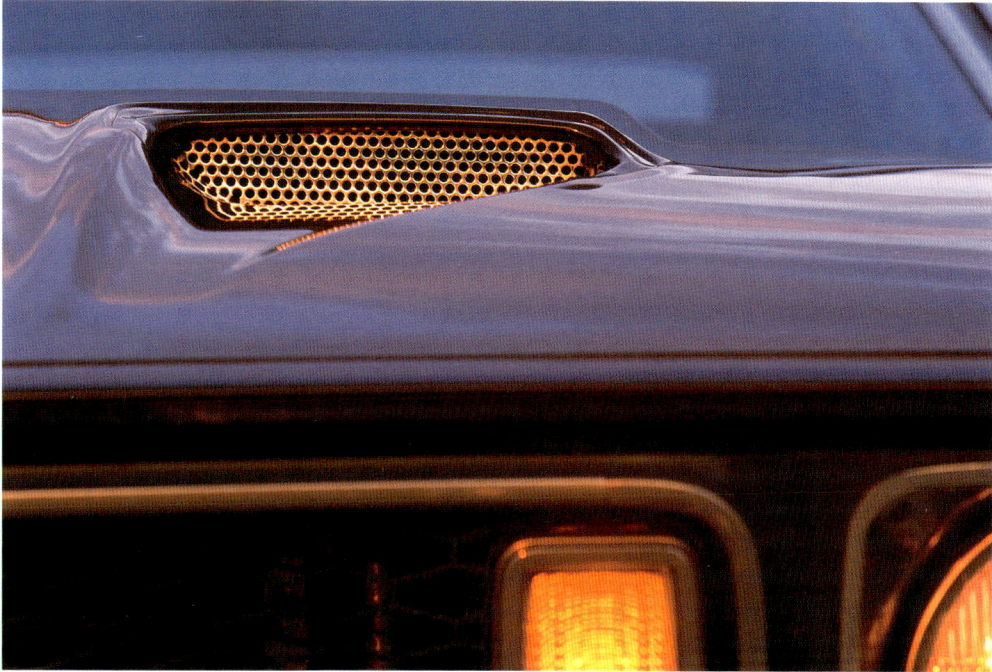

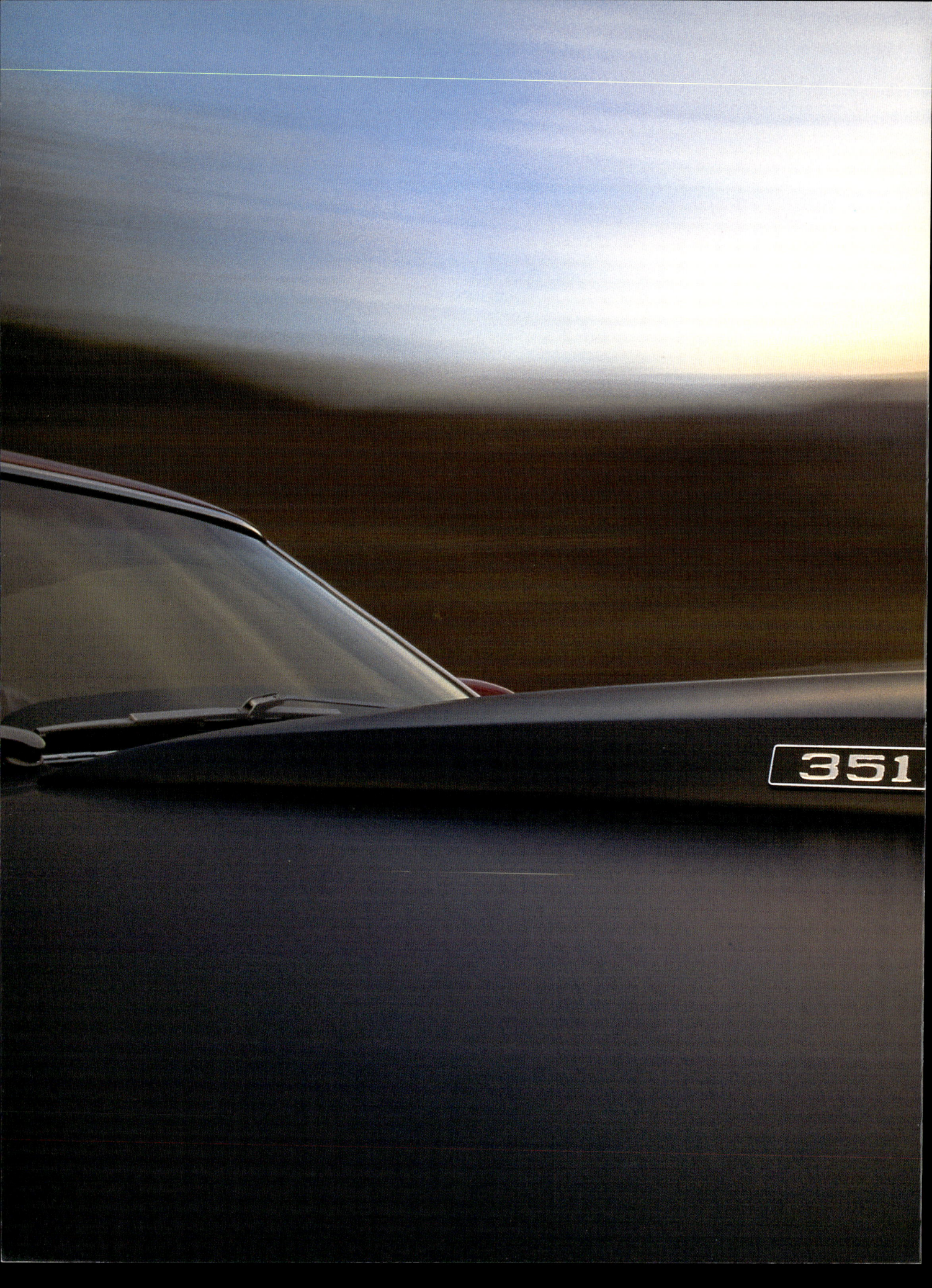

MUSCLE CAR
COLOR • HISTORY

MUSTANG

1964 ½ - 1973

DAVID NEWHARDT

MOTORBOOKS
INTERNATIONAL

This book is dedicated to my uncle,
Richard Bonnefoi,
whose skill behind the wheel led me to grasp it with
both hands and see what was down the road.

This edition first published in 2003 by Motorbooks International,
an imprint of MBI Publishing Company, Galtier Plaza, Suite 200,
380 Jackson Street, St. Paul, MN 55101-3885 USA

Motorbooks International titles are also available at discounts in bulk
quantity for industrial or sales-promotional use. For details write
to Special Sales Manager at Motorbooks International Wholesalers
& Distributors, Galtier Plaza, Suite 200, 380 Jackson Street, St. Paul,
MN 55101-3885 USA.

Library of Congress Cataloging-in-Publication Data

Newhardt, David,
    Mustang 1964 1/2 – 1973 / by David Newhardt.
        p. cm.
    ISBN 0-7603-1187-0 (alk. paper)
    1. Mustang automobile—History. I. Title

TL215.M8N487 2003
629.222'2—dc21

On the front cover: Built to turn as well as it accelerated and braked,
the 1969 Boss 302 was designed to be able to out-handle any comparable vehicle. Wheels such as these were popular aftermarket purchases,
making the standard Magnum 500 15x7 wheels especially valuable.

On the frontispiece: Using the same NASA scoops as in prior years,
the 1973 Mach 1 was little changed from the preceding years, except
for the gradual erosion of power due to mandated emissions regulations. Getting control of emissions required the development of the
EGR system, which allowed for a lean mixture without severe
drivability problems.

On the title page: A nonfunctional scoop on the hood of the 1969
Mach 1 helped convey a sports car image, even though the rear edge
of the piece held turn-signal indicators. Part of the Mach 1's standard
equipment was the Klik-pins attached with lanyards coated with plastic to reduce the chance of scratching the finish.

On the back cover: (top) Introduced in the second half of the 1968
model run, the GT 500KR was the top of the heap. Stuffing the Cobra
Jet engine under the long fiberglass hood resulted in a strong quarter-
mile runner. Total production of the fastback version was 933 units.

(middle) The monochromatic paint scheme was an attempt by Ford to
hold down costs of the 1969 Boss 429. Goodyear F70x15 tires were
standard on the Boss 429, though they stood little chance of handling
the 450 lb-ft of torque at 3,400 rpm.

(bottom) A sleeper in Mustang clothes, this 1973 model is the hot car
for the year. Equipped with a 4-barrel 351-ci engine, it was not possible to get Ram Air with the top engine. 1973 was the first year that
radial tires were available as an option.

Edited by Peter Schletty
Designed by Rochelle Schultz

Printed in China

CONTENTS

ACKNOWLEDGMENTS

As any author will tell you, finding great cars to photograph is easily the hardest part of writing any automotive book. Thankfully, there are enough owners who take justifiable pride in the marque and their cars to provide me with access to a wide array of muscular Mustangs. Their patience with me as I tried to get "just one more" is gratefully recognized.

The following owners deserve far more than I can ever repay for allowing me to lens their cars: Al Bermudez, Alan Bolte, Mark Mosteller, Debbie Taylor, Pete Mendoza, Ben Borla, George Boskovitch, Steve Davis, Siegfried Grunze, Fran Jansen, Bryan Krueger, David Todd, George Chapjian, Courtney Coleman, Jack Green, Rick McGuire, Bruce Meyer, Tony Sousa, William Campbell, Bob Stocker, Jill Johnson, Louis Robinson, Bill and Debbie Sander, Paul Willoughby, Reid Jenson, Richard and Susan Markarian, and Martin Mazman.

Special thanks go to Doug and Marianne Bohrer, whose unflagging pursuit of prime Mustangs and Shelby Mustangs for this book was nothing short of incredible. They introduced me to a wonderful group of owners covering the entire state of California. Best of all, I now count them as friends.

To my old friend Randy Leffingwell, I owe you so much. "Thank you" just doesn't seem enough.

Thank you to Daniel J. Ryan and Jeff Swann at the Museum of Flying at the Santa Monica Airport.

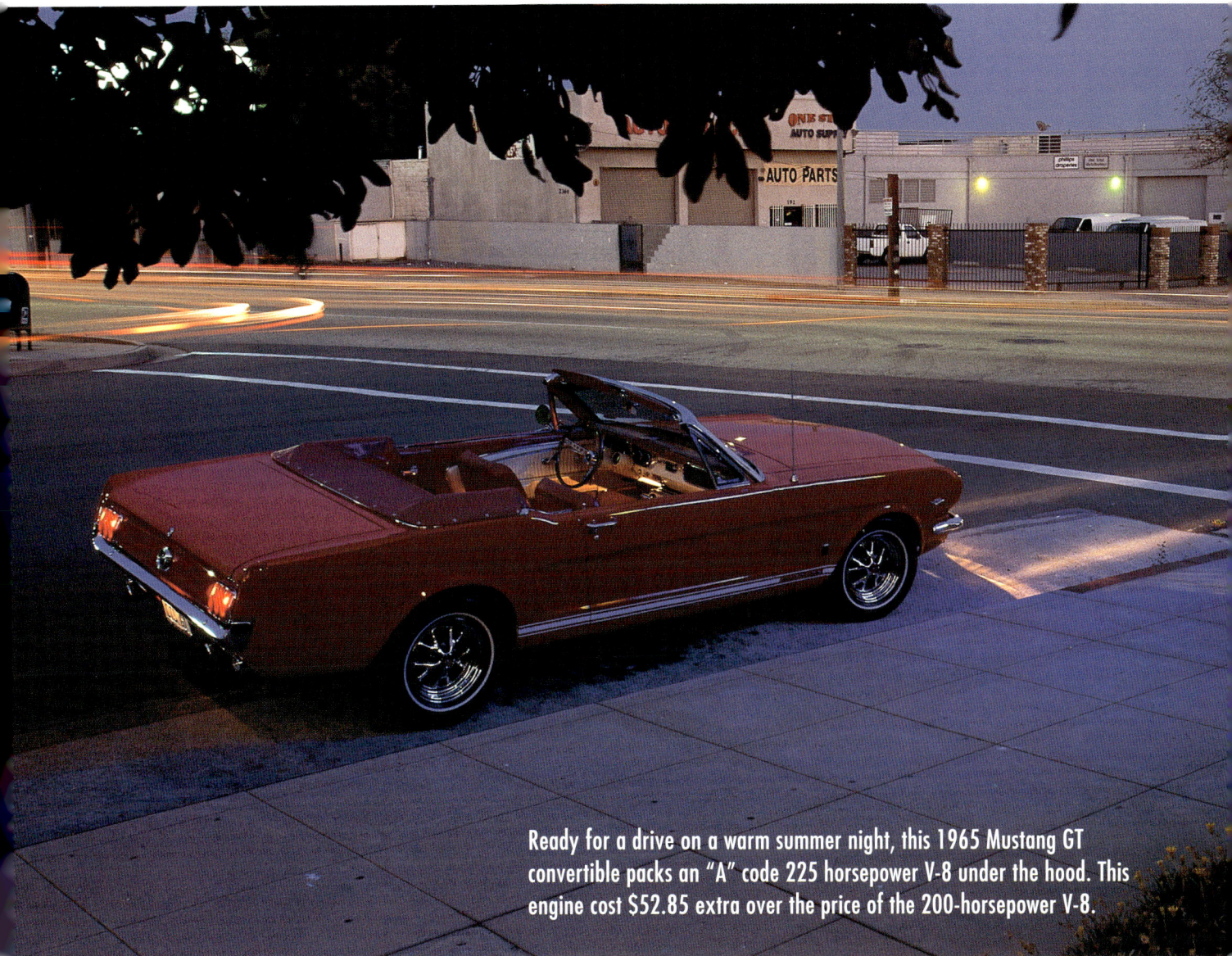

Ready for a drive on a warm summer night, this 1965 Mustang GT convertible packs an "A" code 225 horsepower V-8 under the hood. This engine cost $52.85 extra over the price of the 200-horsepower V-8.

The crew at Motorbooks, laboring in the shadows, deserves a round of applause, especially my editors Peter Schletty, Lee Klancher and Zack Miller.

Last, but by no means least, I want to thank my long-suffering wife Susan, who tolerates my chasing after yet another car to shoot at sunset.

1964 ½ – 1966

CHAPTER 1

BUILD IT AND THEY WILL COME

High performance was part of the Mustang's mystique from the beginning. Image projection is a powerful tool for marketing, and master-marketer Lee Iacocca played the image card for all it was worth. The newest Ford targeted the young and young at heart. General Motors had taken the sedate Corvair and, with the addition of a few simple hop-up parts, turned it into the potent Corvair Monza. The compact dimensions, sprightly performances and modest price resulted in plenty of sales—a clear indication that buyers wanted something different than the leviathans of the late fifties and early sixties. The market was poised for a responsive vehicle that shouted individuality without breaking the bank.

Buyers wanting the hottest Mustang in 1965 ponied up for the famed "K" code engine option. Its 271-horsepower V-8 delivered on its promise of spirited acceleration, getting up to 60 miles per hour in less than eight seconds.

The graceful fastback design was one of three body styles offered when the Mustang debuted on April 15, 1964. The louvers on the C-pillars were functional, a lever inside the car allowing vents to open, improving interior airflow. The dual exhausts were standard with the high-performance "K" code engine.

1965–1967 K-CODE: THE POWER OF A SINGLE LETTER

From its inception around the meeting table at the Fairlane Inn motel in Dearborn, Project T-5 would be a four-seater. Ford was just emerging from the Edsel disaster, and funds were tight. If a new vehicle was going to capture the heart of America, it would have to be on the cheap. Using a production economy car for a significant amount of the mechanical components made financial sense. Iacocca decreed that the new Mustang would weigh 2,500 pounds and retail for under $2,500. The result was essentially old wine in a new bottle. But what lines this bottle had!

Under the Joe Oros/Dave Ash-designed sheet metal was a unibody platform, spun off from the Falcon/Fairlane. The wheelbase was set at 108 inches, enough for a long hood and vestigial rear seats. Forming the basis upon which the suspension and bodywork were hung was

an all-welded frame made up of box-section siderails with five cross-members welded in. Convertibles used heavier-gauge steel and beefed-up reinforcements in the rocker areas. The front suspension consisted of stamped short/long arms, a coil spring attached to the top of each upper arm, and tubular hydraulic shock absorbers housed inside the springs and set into shock towers. It was a simple, inexpensive installation yet responsive to modifications.

While a strong engine isn't really necessary to get a vehicle down the road, the sight and sound of a healthy engine project an image of strength and position. With this in mind, Ford advertised the Mustang for $2,368. That amount of money bought a 170-ci straight six-cylinder engine that generated 101 horsepower. But some people just weren't satisfied with this lofty amount of power.

For those with a beer budget but a V-8 appetite, four paths to additional power were in the option list, from a 260-ci 164-horsepower that went for $116, to the famed K-code 289-ci engine, rated at 271 horsepower and costing $442.60.

Ordering the GT option resulted in a slew of parts being installed, transforming the little pony car into a stallion. Any body style Mustang could be transformed into a GT, but only the 225-horsepower, 289-ci, A-code Challenger Special engine was available in the GT on the April 17, 1964, release date of the Mustang. The GT Equipment Group option was $165.03 well spent. Manual 10-inch front disc brakes, a quicker steering ratio, the Special Handling Package, foglamps set into the grill, chromed exhaust tips, and GT badging and rocker stripes were the ingredients for the GT Package. Instrumentation was upgraded with the GT Package, with the standard horizontal speedometer lifted from the Falcon replaced with circular gauges that said "sports car."

It wasn't until June 1964 that the 271-horsepower version was released. This option, known as the K-code (for the factory engine identification code), was built in relatively low numbers. For the 1965 model year, only 7,273 were built, but they quickly developed a reputation as lightweight, durable, high-output engines.

The K-code engines came about as Ford's response to Chevrolet's excellent small-block. Designed by George F. Stirrat in 1958, it hit the street in 1961, displacing 221 ci. Compact exterior dimensions were a requirement needed for the vehicles that Ford was planning: 8.93 inches in height, 16.36 inches in width, and 20.84 inches in length. It was expanded internally within a couple of years, first to 260 ci, then to 289. It hit its stride at this point, with a thin-wall design, a bore and stroke of 4.00x2.87 inches, and weighing in around 450 pounds. The cast-iron block was fitted with five main bearings to better hold the high nodular iron crankshaft. The connecting rods bolts were a beefy 3/8 inch for high-rpm operation in K-code engines. Topping the block were cast-iron heads, set up for 10.0:1 compression. A cast-iron intake manifold sat under a 400-cfm Autolite 4-barrel carburetor equipped with a manual choke. The carb was topped with a low-profile open-element "racing-type" air cleaner and a chromed cover festooned with a decal denoting output.

Under the chromed air cleaner cover lay a 480-cfm Autolite carburetor, feeding the fuel mixture into a cylinder with 10.5:1 compression ratio. A mechanical camshaft was used, allowing the 289-ci engine to rev up to 6,000 rpm with no adverse effects.

The GT Equipment Group was a $165.03 option and included rocker stripes, fog lamps in the grille, quick ratio steering, manual front disc brakes, and the Special Handling Package.

To keep the valve train in place, screw-in rocker arm studs were installed, and a mechanical camshaft was slipped in. Valve diameters were respectable: intake and exhaust were 1.78 inches and 1.45 inches, respectively. Dual valve springs helped minimize valve float at high revs; and make no mistake, this engine was built to rev. With a bore of 4.05 inches and a stroke of only 2.87 inches, it could spin like nobody's business. This Hi-Po engine was designed to unleash all 271-horsepower at a frenetic 6,000 rpm. Built to operate up to 7,000 rpm, the 289-ci engine used a special 1 13/16-inch-wide harmonic balancer to counteract fourth harmonic unbalance that would become apparent close to maximum revs. Torque was 312 lb-ft, rated at 3,400 rpm. Dual exhausts were fed through cast-iron exhaust manifolds special to the 271-horsepower engine.

All of these enhancements resulted in an engine that Ford knew would see severe service. Rather than cover the engine and powertrain with the standard "24-months/24,000-mile" warranty, the 271-horsepower engine was out of the dealer's hair after only three months or 4,000 miles. Air conditioning was not available with the Hi-Po engine because the compressor belt would be thrown off of the pulley at the speeds the engine was expected to see. On the list of items that couldn't be installed on a 271-horsepower Mustang were limited-slip differential, power steering or brakes, rayon tires, and the three-speed manual transmission.

With the K-code engine, transmission choices in 1965 were easy: a close-ratio four-speed manual. Cruise-O-Matic, Ford's three-speed automatic, absorbed too much power and was not up to durability standards with the increased engine output at that point. A 10.4-inch single dry plate clutch tied the engine and transmission together. In 1966, the Cruise-O-Matic transmission became an option with the K-code engine.

The Special Handling Package was mandatory with the K-code option and was made up of 28 percent stiffer springs, re-valved shocks, and a thicker front anti-roll bar, up from the stock .69 inches

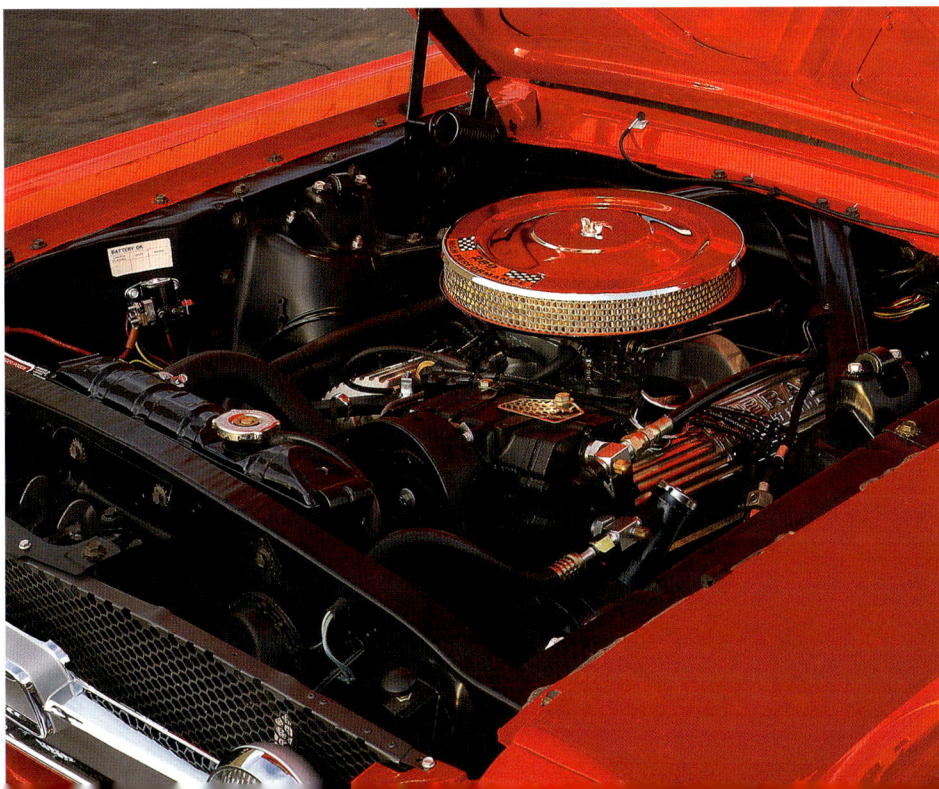

In 1965, most enthusiasts who wanted plenty of power with few worries tended to order the Challenger High-Performance A-code 225-horsepower engine option, a $52.85 premium over the 200-horsepower 289-ci V-8. Only 9.1% of buyers in 1965 bought air conditioning, but more than two-thirds purchased V-8s.

With a "K" code engine, only one transmission was available, a 4-speed manual. Twin instrument pods on the steering column held a tachometer and a clock. The genuine wood Deluxe steering wheel was a $31.52 option, while the pushbutton radio went for $57.51. But the high-winding 289-ci V-8 generated a throaty soundtrack.

to .84 inches. This package was available for only $38, with both the 200- and 225-horsepower V-8s, and worth every dime. The increased power led Ford to install vented 10-inch disc brakes to the front. The rear suspension was almost totally stock Falcon in layout, a live axle with 10-inch drum brakes, but 271-horsepower Hi-Po engines used a 9-inch rear axle ring gear, a step up from the 8-inch unit found in all other Mustangs. Two rear axle ratios were offered, 3.89:1 or 4.11:1. Spring rates for the long asymmetric leaf springs were increased, and 6.95x14-inch Dual Red Band tires were mounted on five-lug 14x5-inch wheels. The standard Mustang's recirculating ball steering used a 21.7:1 steering ratio to provide ocean liner-like steering response, but the Hi-Po K-code package quickened the action of the thin steering wheel with a 16.0:1 ratio. Even with the change in ratios, the Mustang GT took 3.5 turns lock-to-lock, and a turning time of 8.3 seconds was in the ballpark with *Car and Driver's* time of 9.1 seconds with a 235-horsepower 1965 Plymouth Barracuda. The January 1965 issue of *Motor Trend* brought together three other "youth" automobiles in a performance comparison: the Corvair Corsa, the Tempest GTO, and the Barracuda. The turbocharged flat-six of the Chevrolet came up short in this crowd, taking 10 seconds to reach 60 miles per hour. The Barracuda needed 8 seconds to reach the same mark. But the GTO and the K-code Mustang were remarkably close. While the Mustang took 7.6 seconds to work up to 60, the GTO tripped the clock at 7.7 seconds. Quarter-mile performance was closely matched as well, the Ford covering the strip in 15.9 seconds at 89 miles per hour, while the Pontiac did the distance in 15.8 seconds at 93 miles per hour. Even top speed was within a whisker of each other: 114 miles per hour for the Fastback Mustang, 115 miles per hour for the GTO. The Mustang was holding its own.

But Ford didn't want the Mustang to hold its own. They wanted the competition, on the racetrack and in the showroom, to see the triple taillights. If that meant pouring more horsepower under the hood, then so be it. The other manufacturers had made clear that the sales race went to the fleet, and FoMoCo was determined to keep the Mustang in the lead. The K-code option was available through the 1966 model year, but sales of the package slipped badly in the last year to only 472 orders. Buyers could get more bang for their buck with the new big-block engines that were being shoehorned into the Mustang. But that's another story.

circle of 38 feet required three-point U-turns in narrow streets. But U-turns weren't what the Mustang GT was all about.

Performance tests of the day showed that this high-volume Ford could hold its own in sports car circles. *Road & Track* magazine took a K-code to the drag strip for their September 1964 issue and recorded a 15.9-second, 85-mile-per-hour, run down the quarter-mile. Their 0-to-60

Like the namesake airplane, the Shelby Mustang GT350 was an extreme machine, full of raw power and quick reflexes. In either conveyance, allowances were made for its loud, brash behavior, capable of frightening the hand at the controls if handled poorly.

A TEXAN'S VERSION OF A HORSE: 1965–66 GT350

Carroll Shelby was a racecar driver and a darned good one. In the late fifties, he blazed through sports car racing with raw talent and a propensity for promotion. Whether behind the wheel of a Ferrari, Maserati, or anything else with four wheels, the big man from the Lone Star State never lacked the guts to push both himself and others. In 1959, behind the wheel of the Aston Martin DBR1, Shelby and Roy Salvadori won the famed 24-hour race at Le Mans, Shelby racing with a nitroglycerin tablet under his tongue for a heart ailment. He retired from driving race cars in 1960 but was determined to keep a hand in them. With the production of the Cobra in 1962, Shelby forged a relationship with Ford that would prove beneficial to both parties.

Ford knew full well that a performance image helps to sell cars and wanted nothing more than to sell a lot of Mustangs. The high-performance option packages that the factory pitched were well done. But the rube down the street could buy the same tire, shredding 'Stang as anyone else. What Dearborn needed was racing credibility on the cheap. Tooling up for a limited production run of true race-ready Mustangs was simply not an option. Ford contacted the SCCA and asked what it would take to turn the Mustang into a sports car and allow it to race. When the SCCA told Ford that simply putting stiffer springs and a four-speed gearbox on it wasn't enough, Ford turned to the fellow from Texas who had constructed a passel of Corvette-humbling Cobras for far less than it would have cost Ford. His task was to turn the hot-looking Mustang into a hot-running thoroughbred. Enter the GT350.

In order to compete in SCCA events in the B/Production class, a minimum number of race cars needed to be built, in this case one hundred. Ford sent Shelby two Mustang fastbacks, which test driver and engineer Ken Miles and Bob Bondurant evaluated. Following their recommendations, Shelby told Ford that Dearborn would need to send Fastback models with nine-inch rear ends, front disc brakes, and station wagon rear drum brakes with metallic linings, the 271-horsepower engine, and a close-ratio Borg-Warner T-10 4-speed aluminum case gearbox. The V-shaped "export brace" that Ford installed on all Mustangs destined for export was included, helping to triangulate the front suspension and reduce flex.

Once the Wimbledon White "knock-down" (semi-complete) K-code DSO (District Special Option) Mustangs arrived from the San Jose, California, factory to Shelby's shop in the former North American Aviation buildings next to Los Angeles International Airport, his crew went to work transforming the road car into a street-able race car. Instead of a backseat, which wasn't even installed at the Ford factory, a fiberglass panel was fitted with the spare tire strapped down. The steel hood was left off in San Jose and a fiberglass unit with an integral scoop and Klik-pin retainers was installed in its place. Shelby's first employee, Pete Brock, designed the distinctive stripes that instantly identified the GT350.

The bulk of the changes were under the skin. The front suspension was lowered one inch by repositioning the inner pivot points of the upper A-arms.

This tended to increase the camber, which helped to keep the tire upright in heavy cornering. A one-inch anti-roll bar was installed, as well as Koni adjustable shock absorbers. The idler and Pitman arms were lengthened to maintain geometry and increase the steering ratio from the standard 27:1 to 19:1, and a mounted "Monte Carlo" bar ran across the top of the engine connecting the shock towers. Front brakes were massive 11.375-inch Kelsey-Hayes ventilated units

The rear suspension was modified to an equal degree, starting with replacing the stock Falcon rear axle with a shorter but stouter unit from the Galaxie. Inside the large (9-inch) differential were Detroit Automotive no-spin 3.89:1 gears. Another benefit of using the large-car rear axle was the beefy 10x3-inch drum units that received segmented metallic shoes for the anticipated high speeds owners were expected to see. Rear springs were four-leaf, semi-elliptical. In order to keep the axle from misbehaving under load, override traction bars were installed. While effective, their installation required holes to be cut through the floorpan to allow the bars to connect with the brackets. Fiberglass boxes and body filler were used to cover the holes but did nothing to cover the racing intent of the car. A pair of eyelets were mounted above the rear axle with a length of "axle limiting cables" (wire) looped around the rear end, limiting its travel with the rear suspension unloaded. A driveshaft loop was also installed for safety.

A race car is the last place one would expect to see an opulent interior, and the Shelby GT350 did not dispel that line of thought. Available in any color as long as it was black, the interior used standard

Mustang seats in the front. As per SCCA rules requiring the car to be a two-seater, nary a thought was given to a rear seat. In an effort to attain $^{50}/_{50}$ weight distribution, the full-sized spare tire was mounted on the fiberglass cover behind the seats. The final weight split for the GT350 was 55% front and 45% rear, compared to 56%/44% for a stock Mustang. Wide 3-inch seat belts held the occupants in place, the driver holding a 15-inch wooden steering wheel. Atop the center

Mustang radiator was judged insufficient for the task. It was pitched out and replaced with the heftier unit from an air-conditioned Galaxie 500. The regular exhaust was ditched and replaced with Cyclone & Belanger steel tube "Tri-Y" headers, which passed exhaust gases through glass-packed mufflers, then dumped into the atmosphere in front of the rear tires. The battery was installed in the trunk, but after early owners started complaining about fumes and corrosion

In order to stiffen the front suspension of the Mustang, Shelby engineers utilized both the V-shaped "export brace" connecting the shock towers to the firewall as well as the "Monte Carlo" bar running across the front of the engine to tie the towers together. With the 289-ci V-8 tuned to generate a lusty 306 horsepower, the suspension could use all the help it could get. For better weight distribution, Shelby moved the battery to the trunk, figuring few people would use it anyway.

of the Falcon-sourced dash were a pair of gauges: a tachometer and oil pressure. No radio, of course.

The Hi-Po 289-ci, 271-horsepower, engine did not receive any interior modifications, but a handful of goodies kicked up the power. The stock carburetor was tossed out in favor of a 715-cfm center-pivot float Holley on top of an aluminum high-rise intake manifold. High-performance engines tend to generate quite a bit of heat, and the stock

on the inside of the trunk lid, it was back to the engine room for the offending component. A cast aluminum Cobra baffled oil pan increased capacity from 5 quarts to 7.5. The top of the engine was dressed up with cast aluminum valve covers. That was the extent of Shelby's engine changes in the 1965 model. But these few improvements made a difference, with the 10.5:1 compression-ratio small-block generating 306 honest horsepower at 6,000 rpm, and torque coming in at 329 lb-ft at 4,200 revs. The spin-happy K-code was a tough engine, and it welcomed the massaging.

The biggest improvement over the stock Mustang was the handling. At first it might have felt twitchy, but the GT350 was a race car first, a street car second. The controls required a firm effort, but the driver knew that the next gear was engaged. With nary a trace of emission controls, the engine acted like it was wired directly to the driver's will, gathering rpm in voracious quantities, the exhaust note a passable imitation of a Nike rocket. The large 15-inch steering wheel would squirm and buck as the 7.75x15 Goodyear Blue Streaks scrabbled for traction. The GT350 rewarded heads-up driving with rapid travel; a heavy hand would result in lurid slides or worse. Yet enough people wanted the chance to live out a Walter Mitty dream, or actually race, to sell 525 street GT350s at $4,547.

The results were worth the trouble, as Shelby grabbed the SCCA B/Production class in 1965 and never looked back. In 1966 and 1967, privateers raced R-code Shelbys to victory in B/Production. More on that later. What kind of numbers did the GT350 churn up? In the May 1965 *Road & Track*, the stormer was put through its paces. In acceleration, it didn't disappoint, with 60 coming up on the speedometer in 6.8 seconds. The quarter-mile test resulted in the lights being tripped in 14.7 seconds, the Shelby crossing the line doing 90 miles per hour. Top speed was found to be 124 miles per hour, but the optional 4.11:1 gear ratio would have delivered a lower top velocity.

The drag racing model was a rare version of the GT350. Only seven were built in 1965, four in 1966. Designed only

to cover the quarter-mile, it was hoped that the dominance and press that the road racing cars enjoyed could translate into sales to drag racers. Don McCain, Shelby American sales representative and drag racing enthusiast, got together with Max Muhleman, Shelby's Director of PR, on April 9, 1965, to devise a plan to get the GT350 onto the quarter-mile. Shelby approached the NHRA and got a list of necessary modifications to allow the GT350 to run in B/Stock Production against small-block Corvettes.

A car was sent to famed race car builder and engine guru Bill Stroppe, who had a long history of turning Ford products into winners. The engine was balanced and blueprinted, the heads were cc'ed to 44 per cylinder, and a race valve job was done. Large valves were slipped in: 1 $^7/_8$-inch intake, 1 $^5/_8$-inch exhaust. To take advantage of the engine work, a racing camshaft with .272-degree duration and .450-degree lift was available for $90. A set of Belanger drag headers replaced the Tri-Y steel units, while a Hurst Competition shifter was installed in place of the stock unit. A torque strap was attached to control torque twist. Buyers of this optional engine enjoyed warranty-free racing. For 1965, the Koni shock absorbers were pulled off and replaced with Cure-Ride up-lock (90/10) items in the front and Gabriel "Silver Eagles" down-lock (50/50) at the rear. In 1966, the Gabriels were pulled off and Konis installed. The differential was filled with a 5.13:1 gearset in 1965, and a 4.86:1 set in 1966 to aid in quick launches. Stroppe-designed ladder-bar torque arms were fitted to minimize axle hop. Rolling stock was comprised of 14x5 steel wheels surrounded by 9.00x14 rubber in 1965. In 1966, Casler cheater slicks were mounted on 15-inch steel wheels. The best-recorded run from a GT350 was 12.68 seconds. Retail price for all this fun was $5,441.50, with "AFX" rear lift bars as a $200 option.

During model year 1966, Shelby GT350s were changed slightly from the previous year's version. Ford saw that the demand for the GT350 was more significant than they had initially anticipated. While Dearborn made very little on the vehicles it delivered to Shelby American, it did see a financial opportunity. A number of Ford execs paid Shelby a visit and suggested some changes that would keep costs down and increase production. Shelby dealers were clamoring for more user-friendly features such as an automatic transmission, a quieter interior, more exterior colors, and a rear differential that didn't clunk around every slow corner. By utilizing more of the regular Mustang items and cutting out some of the Shelby-only parts, the GT350 would enjoy wider buyer appeal and cost less to produce. Shelby quickly agreed, and "refinements" were instituted. Little did Shelby know that renters would stretch his production facilities thin.

Because of the model year changeover, the first 252 GT350s for the 1966 model year were in fact 1965 vehicles. But running changes were a constant in Shelby-world, and the GT350 was no exception. The traction bars are a good example. About one-third through the 1966 production run, the supply of override bars dried up. Rather than go to the expense of getting more, and continuing to cut holes in the floor pan, a costly and time-consuming procedure, bolt-on Traction Master underride bars were adopted. So it's possible for two 1966 model GT350s to have some significant differences yet both be correct.

The most obvious changes from 1965 were the rear quarter windows made out of Plexiglas and the functional fiberglass rear brake cooling scoops installed aft of the doors. Ducting ran the cool ambient air to the rear drum brakes. Four colors were added to the roster: Sapphire Blue, Ivy Green, Raven Black, and Candy Apple Red. But these hues were only available after the carryover 1965 models were built. For the first time, an automatic transmission, Ford's C4, was made an option, as well as a factory-installed

Paxton supercharger for $670. This rare piece was installed in only 11 vehicles, even if it boosted power by up to 46%. The staff at *Motor Trend* attacked the drag strip with one, coming away with a run of 14.0 seconds at 102 miles per hour. The 90-day/4,000-mile warranty might have been a bit off-putting. The Detroit Locker "no-spin" ratcheting rear end was moved to the option list as a dealer-installed item. Another first for Shelby was the inclusion of the flip-down Mustang rear seat. It was officially an option, but all except 82 of the early cars had it installed. All carryover 1966 cars had their front control arms lowered following 1965 practice, but later vehicles had an unmodified front suspension. Koni shock absorbers were the standard units until vehicle #252. After that, the Konis were a dealer-installed option. Midway through the model year, a radio was offered as a factory-installed option. The two-gauge pod on top of the dash was replaced with a single 9,000-rpm tachometer. Together these changes

The interior was all business, with little to distract the driver from the task at hand. A GT350 at full throttle didn't sound far removed from a Rolls-Royce Merlin 61 V-12 engine.

Shelby changed little in the rear of the 1965 GT350 other than fitting a badge. Realizing that, after all, it was still a street vehicle, the factory Ford radio was left in, figuring that before a sanctioned race, the driver would pull it out.

helped make the 1966 GT350 less expensive than the prior year's car, only $4,428. This was still a lot of money for what the uninformed saw as simply a warmed-over Mustang.

The 271-horsepower engine was left alone when the standard 4-speed manual transmission was installed, but buyers opting for the C4 automatic transmission found that the Holley carburetor was replaced with a 595-cfm Autolite. The exhaust no longer exited in front of the rear tires. A number of states had regulations prohibiting it, and GT350s bound

for those states had full-length pipes even in 1965. But the GT350 was still a raw, brutal car, even with the attempts to make it attractive to a wider audience. Sales were impressive with 2,374 units rolling out the door. But it must be noted that 1,002 of those were sold to Hertz Rental Cars in an effort to spice up their product line and improve the company's visibility. That will be addressed later in this book.

1965 GT350R:
THE "R" STOOD FOR RAW

Ford had an incredibly popular car in the Mustang, yet the marketing mavens in Dearborn knew that the youth of the day looked to performance in their vehicles. The standard K-code was an able runner. But Ford realized that the competing manufacturers were tooling up in a hurry with their answer to the Mustang. Living by the adage "Win on Sunday, Sell on Monday," Ford wanted to take the new pony-car to the next performance level in an arena that the youthful buyers would notice. Sports car racing was growing quickly, and few were better at it than Shelby. As noted earlier, his relationship with Ford had spawned the potent Cobra, so when it came to choosing the organization to highlight the Mustang, Carroll Shelby got the call. With Shelby's background in motorsports, nobody should have been surprised when the GT350s he built to comply with the SCCA's 100-vehicle minimum were pure race cars strongly resembling Mustangs. Shelby assigned Chuck Cantwell, a project engineer on the street

GT350s, to put together the separate assembly line for the R-model. Turning the wrenches were Mike Fangster, Bernie Kretzschmar, and Jerry Schwartz. Labeled the GT350R, that lone letter carried more weight than anyone would have believed.

While the rules stated that at least 100 race cars be built to homologate the vehicle, Ford sent Shelby 110 Fastbacks, about two days' worth of K-code production from the San Jose plant. Upon being transported to SoCal, the engines were taken apart. The heads were ported, polished, and cc'ed. More robust valve springs teamed up with a high-lift mechanical camshaft to allow higher sustained rpm operation. The result was an engine that generated between 325 and 360 horsepower.

Shelbys needed to stop as fast as they went, and dinner-plate-sized front disc brake rotors (11.3 inches) helped to rein in the beast. Flexible ducting fed ambient air to the DS-11 brake pads in an attempt to minimize fade. The backing plates on the rear drum brakes had holes drilled in them in an effort to get cooling air to the

As Shelby American was a bona fide manufacturer, it could install its own Vehicle Identification Number. The plate was riveted to the top of the left inner fender in the engine compartment. This plate stamping shows that it is on a 1965 R-model, serial number 101. The competition R-models were not numbered consecutively, as only 37 were built.

Access to the R-model's 34-gallon fuel tank required opening the trunk using the Klik-pin. The hole for the factory fuel filler pipe was blanked off, and the rear bumper was removed. The top of the rear Plexiglas window was bent down to provide a vent path for air in the interior during a race. Using plastic in this application shaved off 20 pounds.

The heart of the beast, an R-model engine, fed a lot of air into the carburetor plenum, enough to generate in the neighborhood of 350 horsepower. Notice the oversized radiator, necessary for shedding heat during a race. Missing is a fan shroud, as it tended to restrict airflow through the radiator at competition speeds.

binders. Depending on the track configuration, any number of rear axle ratios could be installed and affixed to the 28-spline axles. The suspension was identical to the street GT350s with the exception of different alignment specs.

The interior was advertised as being fireproof. When you take into account the fact that virtually anything flammable in the interior was removed, it was a true enough statement. But the true reason for stripping the insides was to reduce overall vehicle weight. It did come with a roll bar, shoulder harness, fire extinguisher, Plexiglas rear window with a vent at the top, and sliding plastic side windows. The regular driver's seat was replaced with a lightweight fiberglass assembly. Opening the trunk exposed the top of the 34-gallon fuel tank, assembled from the bottom halves of two 16-gallon Mustang gas tanks and fitted with internal baffling.

A heavy-duty radiator was installed along with an engine oil cooler mounted low in the front. A fiberglass lower valance replaced the front bumper and increased airflow to the heat exchangers. Taken together, total weight savings were in the vicinity of 300 pounds, bringing the vehicle's weight to about 2,500 pounds. In pure race car logic, buyers would pay more to receive less. It would take $5,995 to put one of these in a garage. From there, it would only head to a track.

The GT350R was intended for race-track use only. Needless to say, anyone who wanted to pay a $1,500 premium over a regular GT350 (not a cheap car itself at $4,547) for a vehicle they couldn't even drive on the street had to be serious about wanting one. Sales numbers don't do the R-model justice. Only 36 were built. Where else could you walk into a dealership, plunk down your money, and possess a truly competitive, set-up race car that could win on any given day?

From the first time it took to a track (it won its first race entered with Ken Miles at the wheel), the R-models dominated B/Production in SCCA racing in 1965, 1966, and 1967. In the March 1965 issue of *Sports Car Graphic*, Jerry Titus wrote, "Under full power it uses quite a bit of road—a real drifter—but gets a

(continued on page 28)

Shelby replaced the front bumper of the standard GT350 with a molded fiberglass piece on the R-models. Shaped to direct air into the radiator, it was quickly adopted by other racers. Loud, stiffly sprung, with muscle-building steering, the R-model won the SCCA B/Production championship in 1965 and 1966.

BEHIND THE WHEEL
OF THE GT350R

It's one thing to drive a street car that has been modified for competition, and it's another thing to pilot a pure race car. The GT350R is simply a beast.

Never designed to wear a license plate, it lacks the frills most of us are used to, such as carpeting, fancy interior trim, or a muffler. What's it really like?

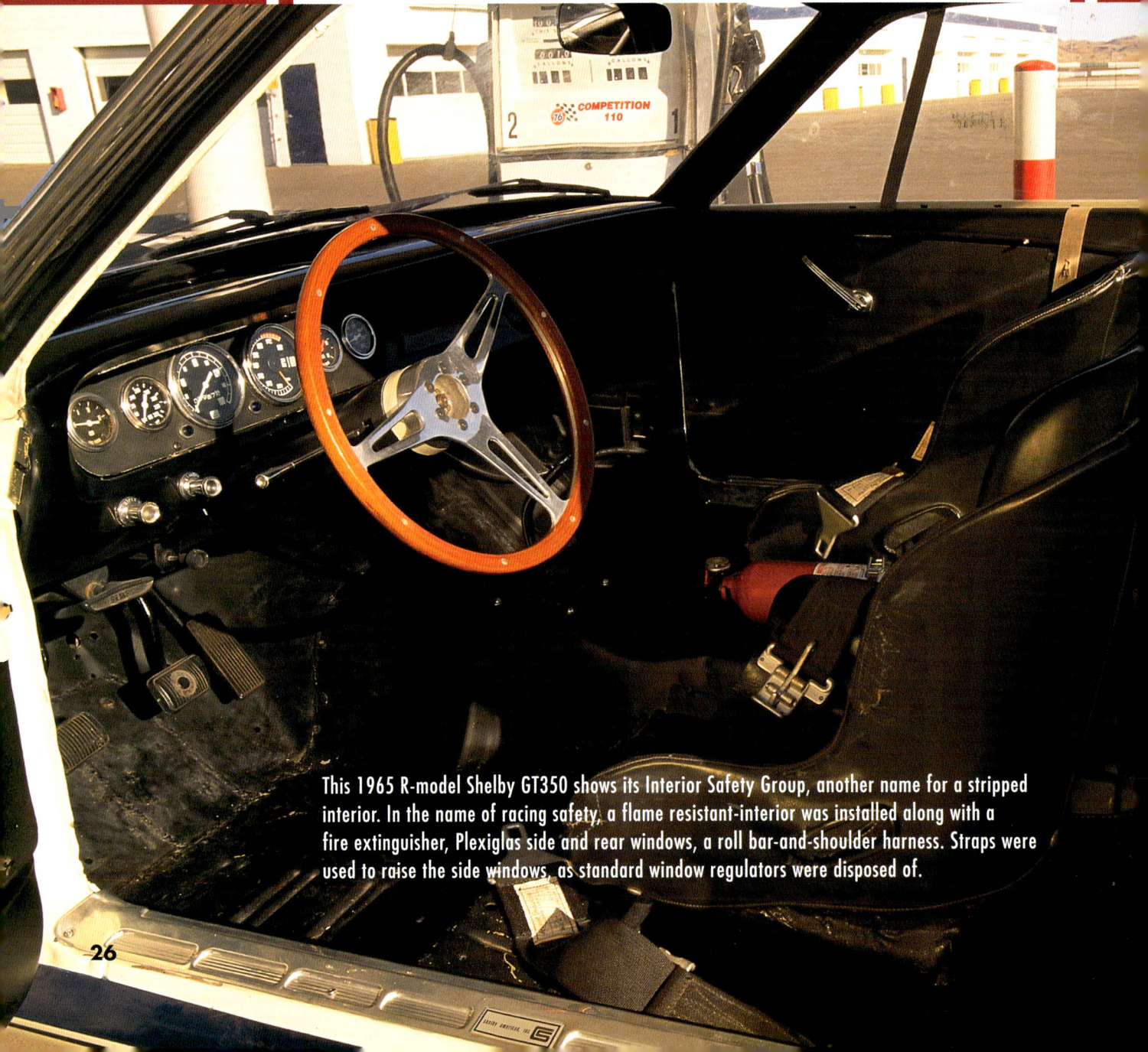

This 1965 R-model Shelby GT350 shows its Interior Safety Group, another name for a stripped interior. In the name of racing safety, a flame resistant-interior was installed along with a fire extinguisher, Plexiglas side and rear windows, a roll bar-and-shoulder harness. Straps were used to raise the side windows, as standard window regulators were disposed of.

Getting behind the wheel is a chore, the tall sides of the racing seat requiring Gumby-like contortions before strapping on the car. Turn the master power switch to on, pump the accelerator a couple of times, then turn the normal Mustang key. The starter whirrs, then a sound like an engine exploding erupts from under the hood. The car starts to vibrate, shaking like a bone in a dog's maw. The exhaust pipes dump buckets of decibels a couple of feet from the ears—the better to hasten deafness. Clutch in, heavy, meaty shifter thunking into first gear, light on the gas pedal. Ease the clutch out, a jolt, then a lurching motion. Easing on the gas, the cacophony rises exponentially as the suspension starts to clunk and shudder. The clutches in the rear end can't seem to make up their minds, banging and jerking as I turn. Check the temps, straighten the steering wheel, and then bury the accelerator. The car leaps forward like its tail has been struck with a hot poker. The tachometer can't come close to keeping up with the spinning under the hood, so shifting by ear is the rule. Before I can say "redline," I grab second gear and push my right foot into the floor. The acceleration doesn't seem any slower in second, or third for that matter. The sound inside is now deafening to the point of silence. Every body panel, every moving part is contributing to the thunderous wave of sound, which I would probably appreciate if I wasn't trying to keep this bucking missile in some semblance of a straight line. Turn ahead—best to get ready well before. I push the brake pedal, but the cold metallic linings interpret my order to slow down as merely a suggestion. Downshift, downshift, turn the wheel a touch, on the gas, weight transfer aft, it hooks up and slingshots down the straight.

So it goes, this subtle, insidious fix for velocity, burrowing deeper into the mind to that place where we're children again and going fast is joy itself. Growing up is greatly overrated.

surprising amount of bite when cornered in a neutral or closed-throttle attitude. The brakes work great in a straight line, but the tail-end is very sensitive if you try the same thing with the wheel turned."

At the end of the 1965 racing season, GT350s were victorious in five out of six divisional championships, and factory driver Jerry Titus was the year's champ. The following year, Shelby pulled out of B/Production to avoid any appearance of the "factory" drivers having an unfair advantage over privately owned vehicles. Shelby was adamant that customer cars were on an equal mechanical footing with factory vehicles. Privateers carried the banner, winning B/Production national titles in both 1966 and 1967. The GT350R flat dominated its class. A number of GT350R models were sold and delivered in 1966, and two were even sold in 1967. But they were, in actuality, 1965 models as noted on their VIN tags. The units that went out the factory door in 1966 used 1966 grilles and rocker panel stripes.

The impact of the 36 GT350Rs produced was far out of proportion to the numbers built. They were intended to be ready to race "out of the box." They

did more than race—they won. Even today, their presence affects Shelby fans as clones of R-models exist by the score. Imitation truly is the most sincere form of flattery.

1966 GT350H HERTZ: MR. MITTY, YOUR CAR IS READY

It's hard to imagine the social climate of the mid-sixties today. What national car rental firm would dream of putting detuned race cars into the hands of Joe Public? Yet that is exactly what Hertz did in 1966 when it put GT350s on its rental car lots. Targeted at mature, well-off, traveling professionals, Hertz knew the program would have a "halo" effect on the entire line of Hertz rental cars. To get the keys at the counter, a renter had to be a member of the Hertz Sports Car Club and willing to ante up $17 a day, or $70 a week, and 17 cents a mile. For the first time in Hertz's history, the automotive enthusiast magazines were writing stories about a real performance vehicle in the company's line-up, rather than just printing ads.

Peyton Cramer, general manager at Shelby American, was aware that the Hertz rental car company was phasing out

Ten-spoke 14-inch cast aluminum wheels were fitted to some GT350H cars, as was the chromed Magnum 500 wheel. Both sported a Hertz center logo.

their program of Corvettes-for-hire. He and Shelby cooked a plan to paint a GT350 in the colors of Mr. Hertz's original rental cars, get it in front of Hertz execs, and see if Shelby American could supply the firm with vehicles to rent through the Hertzs Sports Car Club. A car was prepared and then flown to New York City to be displayed to the suits on November 23, 1965. They loved it and ordered 200, later (December 21, 1965) requesting an additional 800 units, with $300,000 committed for advertising. Pricing was set at $3,547, plus $45.45 for a radio.

Hertz wanted to reduce the amount of abuse these cars would invariably be subjected to by equipping them with C4 automatic transmissions. Rear back seats and a radio were part of the package, as well as the standard GT350 unboosted brake system. Equipped with metallic shoes and pads, they were rather ineffectual when cold, requiring significant pedal pressure to work. A sticker was placed on the dash warning drivers that the brakes didn't respond like a grocery getter. Still, drivers complained. After some early rental customers bent a nose or two trying to stop with cold brake pads, a boosting system was cobbled together, helping civilians to slow the race-bred cars.

While the vast majority of the Hertz GT350s came in Raven Black with Bronze Metallic stripes, upwards of 230 were painted in standard Shelby colors, including green, blue, and red. A handful went into Hertz's hands with no LeMans stripes, making them rare indeed. In model year 1966, the 1,000 GT350Hs (as the Hertz models were designated) made up 40% of Shelby American's business, total production being 2,380 cars.

The scoops in front of the rear wheels were functional, feeding cool air to the rear brakes. The vents in the C-pillar of the 1965 GT350 were replaced with Plexiglas windows to improve visibility.

Only $17 a day, 17 cents a mile. While most GT350Hs were Raven Black with Bronze Metallic stripes, Ivy Green was one of a handful of optional colors, including Sapphire Blue, Candy Apple Red, and Wimbledon White. The 1,001 units built made up almost half of GT350 production of 2,374.

Just because the GT350H came with a rental agreement didn't mean that it couldn't run with the big boys. Under the hood was the same 289-ci V-8, delivering the same 306 horsepower and 329 lb-ft of torque the regular GT350s enjoyed. That figures out to 1.05 horsepower per liter. With the installation of the automatic tranny, the Holley carburetor was replaced with a Ford Autolite 4-barrel. The exhaust was routed from the front of the rear tires to a more passenger-friendly configuration under the rear bumper. Holding occupants in their seats were the wide 3-inch belts favored by WWII fighter pilots. They came in handy, as evidenced by the numbers that Car and Driver generated in their May 1966 road test.

Most GT350Hs rolled on 14x6-inch steel "Magnum 500" wheels, similar to the standard Shelby wheels except for the chromed spokes on the Hertz version. Goodyear Blue Streak tires, 7.75x14, were the best street-performance rubber on the market at the time, yet torque respects no tire. With a 3.89:1 gear set in the differential, the quarter-mile was covered in 15.2 seconds at 93 miles per hour. The popular 0-to-60 test saw 6.6 seconds sweep by on the stopwatch, and top speed turned out to be 117 miles per hour. Extracting that kind of performance took its toll on fuel mileage, and the flashy Hertz consumed one gallon every 6 to 8 miles. But nobody ever drove one with economy in mind anyway.

Unlike 1965 model GT350s with their tachometers in shaped housings, the 1966 editions used a Shelby-labeled tach bolted atop the dash pad. The wooden steering wheel lent a racing touch to the GT350H, but an automatic transmission and radio injected comfort and convenient touches that customers expected in a rental car.

Under the hood, the 1966 GT350H was essentially a carryover from the prior year. Notice that the battery was brought into the engine compartment, as most renters tended to use the trunk to carry items. The 289-ci V-8 still delivered 306 horsepower at 6,000 rpm, enough to thoroughly embarrass any other vehicle on the rental lot.

1967-1968

CHAPTER 2

STAYING AHEAD OF THE CURVE

The race was on in Detroit. It wasn't the sort of competition that one saw and heard on the likes of Woodward Avenue. This invisible battle was for sales numbers, big bucks via the lusting hearts of America's speed-addled youth. Ford had invented the pony car. Surely the cross-town competition wouldn't sit still and let Ford dealers' order books fill up with requests for Mustangs.

Chevrolet was preparing their counterattack in the guise of the Camaro, while the gang at Chrysler decided to inject their Barracuda with some actual performance. The winning formula for drawing wallets into the showroom was to offer big power for small dollars. If that sounds at cross-purposes, consider that the manufacturers had a handful of cards to play and options that could woo buyers with ever growing, gut-wrenching engines with all the subtly of a Saturn V rocket at launch.

What this meant for the consumer was a wonderfully bewildering array of power plants that seemingly generated more of the good stuff for less money. Cubic inches, and lots of 'em, were Detroit's answer. They were already in production and responded well to hop-up tricks. They even cost less than some of the high-output, small-displacement engines in use. And they had a torque curve that looked like

a wave at Sunset Beach—huge. But having big-block engines in the catalog doesn't do much good if they're not in a car.

Ford had a problem. The big-block engines that could take the Mustang to the next level of performance wouldn't fit into the narrow engine compartment. The answer was simple: increase the size of the engine bay to take the next generation of large engines. Except that when an engine compartment is enlarged, the rest of the vehicle must correspondingly grow as well. Suspensions must be beefed up, necessitating a stronger frame and body. This adds weight, meaning more beefing up of the underpinnings. The increased weight of the engine was a considerable factor, as well as the growing number of options that buyers insisted on. Before long, the lithe Mustang had grown into a middleweight. But it was still a contender.

Shelby installed the sequential taillight assembly from the 1965 Thunderbird onto the 1968 GT350 and 500. The air extractor scoops on the C-pillars were functional, as Shelby tended to shy away from useless trinkets.

Most drivers got this view of the 1968 Mustang Cobra Jet. Packing a 428-ci cast-iron engine built for severe duty (racing), its rear tires had a very short life expectancy. The side C-stripe was part of the GT Package, a $147 option that spiced up the Mustang with auxiliary lights in the grill, a GT gas cap and GT wheel covers.

1967 GT390:
CODE "S" FOR SPEED

Mustang shoppers in 1967 got a jolt when they opened the sales brochure: "Bred first . . . to be first." They could now order their image-mobile with a genuine big-block engine. Granted, it was an off-the-shelf item, only a 390-ci model instead of the race-honed 427-ci monster, but it had 320 horsepower. Better yet, it dished out a torrent of torque: 427 lb-ft at 3,200 rpm. And check out the new interior and revised exterior styling! The catalog offered nothing but pure fun.

And fun was what the 1967 'Stang delivered. The Mustang was pouring money into the corporate coffers, and the last thing Ford wanted to do was mess with the golden goose. Ford planners had started developing the 1967 Mustang in 1964 when the decision-makers felt that the public would eventually want more room and power. So the Mustang grew, but in an evolutionary sense.

There was no mistaking the 1967 model for anything else but a Mustang. While the 108-inch wheelbase did not change from 1966, the overall length increased by 2 inches, all of it in the nose. Because of the inclusion of large engines in the line-up, the width of the vehicle was increased by 2.7 inches to 58.1. Height increased by about .5 inch. Ford designers changed the sheet metal from the beltline down. Like the year before, three versions were on the roster: a coupe, a convertible, and a fastback. The latter model was a real head turner, with a greenhouse that swept back to the rear of the body. With a wider body came a larger interior with more of everything, from leg, head, and shoulder room, to freshened instrument panel. Luxury touches abounded, such as red/white door courtesy lights, door ajar and low fuel warning lights, and circular gauges.

Engine/transmission combinations had never been so vast before, with 13 available. From a 200-ci, 120-horsepower, straight six-cylinder to the K-Code 289-ci V-8, 271-horsepower, Ford could match buyer's desires with their wallets. For customers wanting even more, the Dearborn manufacturer pulled an engine out of the company's full-sized lineup to slip under the Mustang's long hood.

The fitting of the "FE" 390-ci engine signaled that Ford was willing and able to go toe-to-toe with anyone else in the horsepower wars. A dependable power-plant, it came on the scene in 1961 and was part of the 352/390/428 family. This engine, with 4.63-inch bore centers, was a deep-skirt design, able to handle displacement increases with ease. Not originally developed as a performance engine, it enjoyed attention from power-seeking engineers in the mid-1960s as an affordable path to street presence. When fitted with a hydraulic cam and a 600-cfm Holley 4-barrel carburetor, the "Thunderbird Special" generated 320-horsepower at 3,600 rpm. More importantly for street performance addicts, torque measured in at a tire-shredding 427 lb-ft. On a horsepower/dollar scale, the big-block had the 271-horsepower, 289-ci engine beat. The high-revving small-block option cost $433.55, but the beefy big-block went for only $263.71. This short-stroke engine (4.05 bore x 3.78 stroke) revved quickly, producing maxi-mum torque at a languid 3,200 rpm. The compression ratio of 10.5:1 meant that premium fuel was required, but the results were worth the extra cost.

In the December 1966 issue, the gang at Motor Trend tested a 390-ci, 4-speed manual transmission equipped model, coming up with a 0-to-60 time of only 7.4 seconds. The quarter-mile test came in at 15.6 seconds at 94 miles per hour. But the staff had a difficult time getting the rear axle to settle down, as the massive torque prompted significant axle hop. Another road test, this time in the January 1967 issue of Car Life, used a 390-ci, 3-speed automatic transmission model, with 60 miles per hour showing up on the speedometer in 7.8 seconds, with the drag strip resulting in a run of 15.5/91.4. They kept the accelerator pedal to the floor

This styled steel wheel was part of the GT Package option and, in a modified form, was the standard wheel on the 1969 Mustang. The Goodyear F70x14 tires were the best tires for the time on a sports car.

and came up with a top speed of 113 miles per hour.

With the increased size came an increase in weight. Curb weight on a big-block model was in the neighborhood of 3,262 pounds, and the Lincoln Continental–sourced 11.38-inch Kelsey-Hayes front disc brakes were put to the test. In Motor Trend's review, the vehicle came to a stop from 60 miles per hour in 134 feet, a respectable distance. Tires were F70 Firestone Wide-Ovals, state-of-

In 1967, Shelby had to design a more aggressive look for the GT350 because the standard Mustang for that year had more aggressive lines. Built in very limited numbers, the GT350S used a Paxton supercharger to boost power upwards of 150 horsepower.

the-art for the day, mounted on 14x6-inch wheels. Larger 15-inch wheels were available as part of the $388.53 Competition Handling Package. This set-up included a stiffer suspension, Koni adjustable shocks, a limited-slip differential, 670x15 Super Sport tires, and quick 16:1 manual steering. Buyers could order this option as long as they had a 390-ci or a 289-ci engine with 271 horsepower under the hood. The result was a ground-hugging auto that made sure you felt every bit of the road. Three rear axle ratios were available, 2.80, 3.25, and 3.50:1. With the introduction of the 3-speed Select Shift Cruise-O-Matic automatic transmission, a buyer could

tailor the engine and transmission to the job at hand, whether it was scorching stoplight performance or effortless high-way cruising.

The large engine tipped the scale some 200 pounds heavier than the 289-ci small-block, and when taking a corner with verve, physics will not be denied. To help reduce the effect of the iron block heavyweight, Ford fitted the Mustang with a 0.72-inch stabilizer bar and 125 lb/in front springs, upgraded from the standard small-block 103 lb/in units. The rear springs were left alone on all Mustangs, regardless of engine, measuring in at 110 lb/in. Ordering the big-block also saw a slightly smaller fuel tank

installed holding 16 gallons, unlike the 17-gallon unit installed on six-cylinder and small-block V-8 models.

Big-block Mustangs, with 58% of their weight on the front tires, were more at home in a straight line than chasing a winding road, but improvements in the steering system helped the 1967 model get around a corner. In the November 1966 issue of *Car and Driver,* the editors wrote that "the Mustang corners willingly, if somewhat clumsily. It doesn't seek the right line instinctively, the way a thoroughbred will, but once pointed in the proper direction, it clambers eagerly around the corner." With the use of low-friction steering joints and a revised front suspension, the manual steering ratio was improved to 25.3:1, while the power steering setup further improved the ratio to 20.3:1.

With improvements in controlling noise, vibration, and harshness, such as the fitting of polyethylene-filled ball joints, the Mustang was well on its way to becoming a Grand Tourer rather than a sports car. The top engine option in earlier years, the 271-horsepower small-block, sold only 472 units for 1967, while 28,800 buyers opted for the torque-heavy big-block. Customers wanted maximum grunt for minimal dollar, and the Mustang 390 was a bargain. The equation was simple: For velocity, check "Code S."

Grasping the thin wooden steering wheel in a 1967 GT350S could be a very humbling experience. The beefy Hurst shifter demanded a firm movement, leaving no doubt that another gear had been engaged.

1967 SHELBY GT350: MORE OF EVERYTHING

It stood to reason that with a revamped Mustang hitting the showroom for 1967, the shrewd bunch at Shelby American would turn up the temperature. Carroll Shelby was dividing his time between his West Coast factory and the English race shops that were preparing the GT40s that would assail LeMans. He knew that he couldn't duplicate the transformation of the street Mustang into

Filling the front left corner of the engine compartment, the air cleaner for the 1967 Shelby GT350S was the size of a large coffee can. It pulled in air directly from the grill. This performance enhancing option cost $549 and gave acceleration on par with a big block engine.

a race, winning Shelby GT, so he took what Ford handed him and made the best of it. Sure, the 'Stang grew dimensionally, but Shelby rolled with the changes and introduced two versions to appeal to the widest range of buyers. The GT350 was a direct evolution of the lithe, road-able race cars that made Shelby's reputation in SCCA B-Production. Where the original GT350 tended to rearrange one's internal organs on a long drive, the move to a more street-friendly vehicle was bound to

attract more mainstream customers. As Ford Stylist Chuck McHose recalls in Wallace A. Wyss's *Shelby's Wildlife*, **"Shelby had modified the suspensions on the 1965s and 1966s and the things rode like a truck. People drove them because they thought they wanted a race car but then they found out a real race car is a pig to drive. And yet people wanted them because they liked the image of driving a 'race car.' So Shelby went to Ford's Marketing Department and they told him what people really want is a car that's real easy to drive but looks like a race car."** But make no mistake, the 1967 Shelby GTs were capable of savage performance.

While the early GT350s used the Mustang as a basis for enhancements, the 1967 model leaned quite a bit more closely to the standard Mustang. Unlike the first year's vehicles with major revisions to both front and rear suspensions, the 1967 version was basically a standard Mustang except for the use of heavy-duty, Shelby-specific front springs and a thicker front stabilizer bar. The shock absorbers were upgraded to more affordable Gabriel heavy-duty adjustable units with the export brace still installed. The Monte Carlo bar was no longer used.

Some complained of the larger body when they saw the 1967 Mustang, saying that the vehicle had lost its trim proportions. Shelby used the enlarged form as a starting point to design a road car that was even more over the top than the 1966 model. Ford loaned Shelby one of their stylists, Chuck McHose, who worked with Pete Stacey and Shelby's own Pete Brock to redesign the Mustang. They were tasked with penning a distinctive Grand Tourer that could evoke some of the old road-racing magic while treat-

ing the occupants better than in years past. While the stock 1967 Mustang saw a two-inch longer nose than the 1966, Shelby used fiberglass parts to extend the GT model's proboscis an additional three inches, while sinking the grille farther back. At the back end, three fiberglass pieces were attached to the fastback body style to create a massive rear spoiler. Taillights lifted off the 1967 Mercury Cougar, complete with the sequential turn-signal feature, flanked a center fuel cap emblazoned with the Shelby logo. Early cars had twin high-beam lamps at the centerline of the grille, mimicking a race car.

Ford sent a group of engineers to Shelby's Los Angeles plant to assess production. One of the Ford staff, Fred Goodell, could not believe the lack of standard production procedures. After he got the line up to speed, he went to

Sacramento to find out that center-mounted headlights, as well as red lamps mounted in the C-pillar air extractor scoops, were not legal on non-emergency vehicles. The many fiberglass pieces that turned a Mustang into a Shelby were of such abysmal quality that the handiwork required to get an acceptable panel-fit made the Shelby work floor look like an assembly line from half a century earlier. Approximately 200 autos had been assembled by that point, so a redesign of the grille was done, moving the high-beam lamps outboard. That, in turn, improved airflow into the radiator, keeping engine temp within norms.

Inspired by the GT40, functional scoops festooned the GT350. The rear quarter scoops fed air to the rear brakes in early cars, but as supplies were used up, the scoops turned to appearance items only. Functional throughout the entire

A roll bar with inertia reel shoulder harnesses helped to stiffen the Shelby GT350S body structure as well as provide a level of safety not found in standard Mustangs. Shelby did not scrimp when it came to badges, both the interior and exterior festooned with them.

39

Center-mounted driving lamps may have been a stylistic hit, but they conflicted with a number of states' lighting codes. Only early 1967 Shelby Mustangs featured this lamp configuration. Later vehicles mounted the lights at the outboard ends of the grill to comply with regulations. This, in turn, improved engine cooling.

production run were the air extractor scoops on the C-pillars, operated by a lever inside the vehicle. The largest scoop on the GT350 was also the most important, as it fed air to the 289-ci V-8 under the long hood.

That power plant was the same sweet-heart of an engine as in the 1966 GT350. Still rated at 306 horsepower, it used solid lifters to attain accurate valve actuation at high rpm's. Early GT350s used a S2MS Cobra high-rise aluminum intake mani-fold to cover the lifter valley, while later vehicles were equipped with an S7MS model. A 715-cfm Holley R-3259 center-pivot float four-barrel carburetor with vacuum secondaries was installed, but the Tri-Y headers of old didn't make it into the engine compartment. Instead, stock Mustang iron 271 Hi-Po exhaust mani-folds fed gases into dual pipes, exiting under the stock rear bumper. At the

bottom of the engine was a stock Ford oil pan, replacing the attractive aluminum Cobra component of years past.

Available as an option was a factory-installed Paxton supercharger for $549. Belt-driven, it boosted engine output in the neighborhood of 100 horsepower. A rare accessory, it is extremely desirable today.

Two transmissions were available: a top-loader four-speed manual, and a C4 three-speed automatic. The manual box used a twenty-eight spline shaft and a 10.5-inch single-plate dry clutch for strength, while the rear axle ratio was dependent on transmission choice. Order the 4-speed and the pumpkin was filled with a 3.89:1 gear, while automatic-equipped GT350s used a 3.50:1 gear set. Only a handful of 1967 GT350s were fitted with the optional Detroit Locker-type "No Spin" limited-slip option. But other options were available over the counter, such as a LeMans Kinetic Superflow Solid Lifter Camshaft Kit for $90.

Even if the trick camshaft wasn't installed, the standard Shelby GT350 engine could definitely get out of its own way. In March 1967, *Sports Car Graphic* put the whip to one, coaxing a 0-to-60 time of only 7.1 seconds. A pass down the quarter-mile netted a 15.3-second/91 mile-per-hour run, while a two-pass top speed run came in at 129 miles per hour. Average mileage was observed at 15 miles per gallon, but frankly, that was the least of a driver's concern. Steering clear of the local law enforcement might rate a higher priority. The editors at *Road & Track* ordered a 1967 GT350 with an optional 4.11:1 rear axle ratio, and the Shelby leaped to 60 miles per hour in only 6.3 seconds. The enthusiast magazines did warm to the handling of the GT350 as long as the options were pared down to a minimum. Understeer, long a designed-in handling characteristic from Detroit products, was still in attendance in the GT350. But the firmer shocks helped the driver feel what the suspension was actually doing and, of course, a touch of throttle could induce the rear end to slide on cue.

All GT350 interiors received the Deluxe Mustang version, which included brushed aluminum door inserts and dash trim. Shelby did not ignore the inside, bolting a four-point roll bar in early cars, changed to a two-point later. For the first time in a production vehicle, the GT350 was equipped with inertia reel shoulder harnesses patterned off the belts used in the F-4 Phantom II fighter. Interior color choices were rather thin, black and parchment; however, some vehicles hit the street with a white cockpit. For the first time in a Shelby, the instrument panel used a 140-mile-per-hour speedometer and an 8,000-rpm tachometer. As a grudging acknowledgment to the increasing buyer preference toward comfort, Selectaire air conditioning was on the option sheet for $356.09.

The twin stripes running the length of the body were a $34.95 option on the 1967 Shelby GT350. Shelby replaced the factory Mustang gas filler cap with one of his own design, a pop-open affair.

The public response to the GT350 was 1,175 sold, about one third of the total volume from Shelby that year. With a base price of $3,995, it was not the cheapest hot car on the road, but it did point the way to Shelby's future, embracing image over racing reality. A buyer might not race the car, but they looked like they could.

1967 SHELBY GT500: THE TRACK'S IN THE OTHER DIRECTION

While the GT350 could trace its lineage directly to the nimble, trophy-winning race cars from 1965, the GT500 was an answer to a marketing problem. Ford and Shelby could see that the horsepower war was just getting started between the American manufacturers, and the quick, cheap solution for tire-melting performance was to slip a big-block engine under the hood. Lightweight, high-revving, small-displacement mills were ideal for a pure racing environment, but the demands of the consumer dictated that creature comforts be mixed with aggressive styling, with a touch of brutality tossed in for good measure. Buyers wanted the aura of racing without the sacrifice. They weren't about to live without the power accessories they had grown accustomed to, such as steering, brakes, and windows.

With luxury comes weight, and to counter the pounds while keeping up with other Detroit manufacturers, Shelby plucked the 486-pound, 428-ci Police Interceptor engine off the shelf, massaged

a few parts, and slipped it under the long fiberglass hood. Because some car companies used engines as large or larger than the 428-ci powerplant, Shelby decided to use the GT500 moniker simply because it was bigger than anyone else's. It delivered the antidote to excess weight: excess torque.

GT500s had a seriously large hunk of iron over the front wheels. Externally similar to the famous 427-ci V-8 that lurked in the GT40, the internals were significantly different. Some earlier customers had complained about the solid lifter-valve clatter, so the 428-ci engine used hydraulic lifters and a "Police Interceptor" camshaft, and had a dissimilar bore and stroke from the race engine, 4.13x3.98 inches. The wide bore and short stroke meant that torque would pour forth on cue, 420 lb-ft at 3,200 rpm. Horsepower was healthy as well, 360 horsepower at 5,400 revs.

Shelby used improved induction to generate more power by the tried and true method of getting as much fuel and air into the cylinders as fast as possible. The compression ratio was 10.7:1, making premium fuel use mandatory.

Topping the large 428-ci heads in a 1967 GT500, these aluminum valve covers hid the overhead valve train used to make 355 horsepower. More useful in street matches was the 420 lb-ft of torque, helping the speedometer swing up to 60 miles per hour in only 6.7 seconds.

The iron block sat under an aluminum dual-plane medium-riser intake manifold that held two 600-cfm 4-barrel Holley carburetors. The front carb was a model R-2804, while the rear unit was an R-2805. They were mounted facing the rear and used a unique linkage to tie them to the accelerator pedal. A long-finned oval aluminum air cleaner topped the carbs, matching the alloy valve covers. With light throttle, the engine operated on the front carb's two primary barrels only. But mash the gas pedal into the carpet, and the remaining six barrels poured high-test into the cylinders like you owned stock in Sunoco. The pistons and crankshaft were cast iron, but the connecting rods were forged steel to help the engine survive the abuse Shelby knew these cars would see.

Two transmissions were available, a 4-speed manual and the beefy C-6 Cruise-O-Matic 3-speed automatic. The rear axle ratio was dependent on the transmission. Order the manual, and the differential was filled with 3.50:1 gears, or 3.25:1 with the automatic. Suspension components were standard for the era, meaning unequal-length A-arms, coil springs, and tube shocks in the front, and a live rear axle, leaf springs, tube shocks, and trailing arms in the rear.

Shoehorning a Police Interceptor 428-ci engine into the 1967 Shelby Mustang resulted in the GT500, a bellowing beast of a car in a straight line. Shelby made 2,048 of them, charging $4,195 each.

Designed by Shelby stylist Pete Brock, the lower sill stripes were so popular that Ford used them later on its production Mustangs. Ten-spoke 15-inch Shelby wheels were offered in the latter half of the 1967 model year.

In a cost-cutting move, the Koni shocks of prior years were replaced with Gabriels, and traction bars were notable by their absence. What Shelby called "rebound dampers" were just rubber bumpers mounted 8 inches behind the front ends of the springs to tame the rear-axle hop that reared its ugly head during hard acceleration. In the February 1967 issue of *Car and Driver*, they pointed out, "The front suspension geometry was determined by Klaus Arning using the same computer he used in setting up the suspension of the Ford GT40." Punch cards, indeed.

Punching the throttle, like *Road & Track* did in their February 1967 issue, generated good performance numbers. On the drag strip, the quarter-mile roared by in 15.5 seconds at 95 miles per hour. It took 7.2 seconds to see 60 miles per hour, while 80 miles per hour took an additional 3.8 clicks. With 15x6.5-inch wheels and E70-15 Goodyear Speedway 350 tires, finding traction with the massive amount of torque was the tricky wicket. With such a nose-heavy configu-ration, it was thought that massive understeer would be on tap, but the handling wizards at Shelby knew how to coax a car around a corner, even one that was built primarily to excel between them. Spring rates in the front were 360 lbs-in, with the rear springs using 135 lb-in, and a .94-inch stabilizer bar installed in the front. The result was a Shelby that, while it didn't cling to an apex like a leech, would embarrass a standard big-block Mustang without even breaking a sweat.

The GT500 was a guaranteed head-turner, thanks to the swoopy bodywork modifications penned by Chuck McHose and Pete Stacey. As Wallace Wyss notes in his book *Shelby's Wildlife*, "'When Shelby came and looked at our life-size mock-up,' recalls McHose, 'he said that the front end "wasn't enough," so we went ahead and deepened the grille cavity as in one of our drawings. Then Pete Stacey had the idea of putting the high beams in the center. After all, no one had ever said quad headlamps had to be in pairs. Shelby liked the idea because he thought it would make the car real distinctive at night.'" Two problems cropped up with the center-mounted lamps: they tended to reduce airflow to

the radiator, and they weren't legal. About 200 cars were built with the lamps in the center of the grille before they were moved to the outboard ends.

Other body mods consisted of scoops on the sides and the C-pillars. A large Kamm-style tail spoiler was fitted above taillamps sourced from the Ford Cougar. The obligatory rocker panel tape stripe let passers-by know that the driver was willing to spend $4,195 to style down the road. A functional scoop fed cool air into the engine bay, but the amount of heat the massive engine produced did nothing

for the dimensional stability of the fiberglass hood. The fiberglass parts were sourced from firms on the West Coast, and the quality was marginal at best. This was a problem that plagued Shelby for quite a while, until Ford started using a fiberglass source close to Detroit in Canada. Which brings up another matter . . .

In the old days, say 1963, when Shelby was building Cobras in relatively small numbers, a handful of dedicated craftsmen assembled each vehicle by

(continued on page 50)

Set in the doorsill tape stripe, the GTA badging indicates that this model is equipped with an automatic transmission.

1967 FASTBACK

Part of the GT option in 1967 was a twist-off gas cap with a GT logo. Triple taillights continued a visual tradition started with the very first production Mustangs.

For 1967, the Mustang used a set of pronounced faux scoops in front of the rear tires. This fastback GT model is fitted with a set of period aftermarket wheels.

Fastback Mustangs in 1967 used manually operated vents in the C-pillars to help with interior ventilation. Like most American vehicles in the 1960s, the interior trim was styled with looks in mind, not safety.

Packed with innovations such as fuel injection and independent rear suspension, the EXP500 is one of the most valuable Shelby's created. It was never meant to get into the hands of the public. Fortunately, Fred Goodell had the clout to hang on to it after it had been evaluated, and today a collector treasures this rolling rarity.

ONE OF ONE:
EXP500

Ever since the first Mustang rolled down the assembly line, there had been people in Ford engineering who felt that an independent rear suspension (IRS) would be the best thing for the pony car. Besides improving the ride quality, an IRS would allow the rear suspension to track over road irregularities at speed, resulting in superior handling. The problem was a familiar one—the bottom line. When the Mustang debuted in April 1964, sales went through the roof; and as the years went on, the public continued to snap up the original pony car. The Ford finance people felt that little would be gained by installing IRS on a vehicle they could barely meet demand on. So the axe went down on that engineering proposal.

But when did the price of anything slow down the gang at Shelby American? In David Friedman's excellent book, *Remembering the Shelby Years—1962–1969*, Shelby project engineer Fred Goodell recounts the birth of one of, if not the rarest, Mustang/Shelbys in existence. "We took a new California Mustang that was shipped to us by Ford and put on Shelby chassis parts plus some new stuff like independent rear suspension, experimental fuel injection, special transmission, and a bored-out (to 456 ci) 428 engine. Plus, it had all the features that the 1968 Shelby had. That car was called 'The Green Hornet' because of its wild paint job. That car turned up, for

real, a couple of years ago, after we'd all thought it had been scrapped many years before. I was the one who wrote out the scrap order on that car, but all of the numbers, including the engine number, matched my engineering records, which I still have today."

With the Shelby snake emblem on the C-pillar of the vinyl roof, the EXP500 looks, at first glance, like a cobbled version of what a Shelby-ized hardtop might look like—except that this is the real deal. It is fitted with all of the period Shelby parts plus an independent rear suspension and a trick fuel injection setup. Today the EXP500 uses a conventional carburetor, but the innovative induction system is in the hands of the vehicles' owner.

In a brief ride in the EXP500, the improvement in ride quality is immediately evident, the body maintaining its poise even after rolling over the road's imperfections. With the massive 428-ci engine under the long fiberglass hood, canyon carving could have been tackled with greater enthusiasm than with a solid-axle car. But costs really did play a role in keeping IRS out from under the Mustang platform until the late 1990s. The EXP500 is one of those rare automobiles that really lets us see what would have happened "if only."

Using taillights from the 1967 Mercury Cougar, the 1967 GT500 oozed attitude. The large rear spoiler was a Shelby piece, as were the scoops on the C-pillar and side.

Shelby touches abounded in the 1967 GT500. While the dash was standard Mustang, the horn button was just one of many places the Shelby factory displayed the company logo. This was the last year for a steering wheel of this design, as safety regulations coming in 1968 required a padded wheel.

hand. Fast forward a few years, and Shelby was trying to put together thousands of cars each year using the same techniques. The Los Angeles facility was strained, big time. Then in 1967, the lease on the building ran out. Ford, who had been watching the labor-intensive assembly process with no small amount of disbelief, decided that they could do a better job building Shelbys than Carroll could. So the making of GT350s and 500s headed East, closer to a source of high-quality fiberglass and modern vehicle assembly procedures. Production of the last one hundred autos took place at the A.O. Smith Inland, Inc. facilities in Ionia, Michigan, later shifting to the Mustang's Metuchen, New Jersey, plant. At the end of the model year, 2,048 GT500s were built.

On the road, the GT500 was a transformed animal compared to the GT350s of the preceding years. While the race-bred small blocks felt like they wanted to dive toward the nearest corner at every chance, the big-block exuded a smoother, more civilized demeanor. This isn't to say that the GT500 would ever be confused with a Thunderbird, but the change in focus was clear. Cruising, albeit at high speed with occasional bursts of frenetic wheelspin, showed that Shelby built something besides sophomoric sports cars. It was now clear that Dearborn was determining the direction that Shelby's modified Mustang was going to take, and it wasn't toward a racetrack. More than ever, the GT really stood for Grand Touring, in the European sense, where a long day's journey would find the vehicle's occupants under a porte-cochere.

1968 COBRA JET: A LITTLE OF THIS, A LITTLE OF THAT

Sometimes good ideas come from the darnedest places. And fate has a funny way of getting one's attention. It was 1968, and Ford dealer and drag racer Bob Tasca was looking for a path to more power. Using some parts sitting on a shelf, he cobbled together a new engine

ribbing in the main web area for strength. Sitting in the five main bearings was a cast-iron nodular controlled crankshaft, machined to deliver a 3.984-inch stroke using connecting rods from the Police Interceptor Package. The crank was held in place using two-bolt main bearing caps, but beefy $^{13}/_{32}$-inch bolts held the parts together. At the other end of the

Starting in 1967, the Shelby Mustangs started to step away from the pure racing car with a license plate to a Grand Touring car that could challenge virtually any street-legal automobile. Installing a large engine over the front tires tended to compromise handling, but it made impressive acceleration numbers.

using a 428-ci block as a start. As both the 428 and race 427-ci engines came from the same FE family, they used identical bore spacing. From the race engine, he installed a pair of 427-ci heads and found power aplenty. Famed drag race driver "Dyno" Don Nicholson put his talent to use and pulled a quarter-mile run of 13.39 seconds at 105 miles per hour. Ford took one look at this hybrid and got the ball rolling to build a new engine from old parts.

Ford started with their Police Interceptor 428-ci block casting, adding extra

con rods were slipper-skirted, cast, flat-topped pistons that slid in a 4.130-inch bore. Above the cylinders was a set of 427-inch cylinder heads. These high-performance heads used a combustion chamber of 72.8–75.8 ccs, which was left in a rougher cast finish. While they used a mechanical camshaft on the race engine, in this application the hydraulic camshaft from the 390 GT engine fit the bill. Specs for this bumpstick were rather subdued, with a lift of .481 inches on the intake valves working with the .490 inches of lift on the exhaust side.

Speaking of valves, their size was not unusual, with 2.09-inch-diameter solid Silchrome intake and 1.66-inch forged steel exhaust. Rocker arms were non-adjustable, shaft-mounted, nothing fancy. However, the intake and exhaust ports were quite a bit larger than the old 390 castings. The compression ratio was 10.6:1.

The use of a cast-iron intake manifold might be construed as anti-performance, especially when it tipped the scale at 90 pounds. But the goal of this engine was to generate large amounts of power on the cheap. So iron on top it was. Luckily, it was a quality designed high-rise style that let a lot of gases flow through quickly. On top of it was a 735-cfm Holley 4150-C two-float four-barrel carburetor, crowned with a single snorkel air cleaner and a chrome lid.

Unlike the restrictive exhaust manifolds found on the 390, the Cobra Jet engine used a set of free-flowing cast-iron header-design manifolds. These used a unique bolt pattern, restricting their use to CJ engines only. From there, exhaust gases found their way to the rear of the vehicle via dual exhaust.

The result of all this Rube Goldberg-type engineering was a tough, strong power plant that didn't cost an arm and a leg. In order to fly under the radar of the increasingly vocal insurance companies, Ford rated the engine at 335 horsepower at 5,600 revs. Sure, it put out that kind of

Filling the engine bay of the 1968 Mustang, the Cobra Jet option put a very big stick in the hands of the driver. Capable of ripping off 0-to-60 runs under six seconds, its rating of 335 horsepower was a gross understatement by the factory.

power . . . on its way toward 400 horse-power. Torque was even hairier, 440 lb-ft at 3,400 rpm. And it didn't take a rocket scientist to employ some basic hop-up tricks to extract more, a lot more.

To qualify the Cobra Jet engine in sanctioned drag racing, Ford built a special run of CJ race cars to be put into the hands of worthy racers. The result was Super Stock Eliminator success. Unleashed for the first time at the early-February Winternationals at the Pomona, California, drag strip, they got noticed, big time. Al Joniec went up against "Dyno" Don, taking the victory in only 12.5 seconds. *Hot Rod* magazine ran the strip to good effect, tripping the lights in 13.56 seconds at 106.64 miles per hour.

Sixty miles per hour came up on the speedometer in only 5.9 seconds. Ford was so proud of the Cobra Jet that it used *Hot Rod*'s data in a full-page advertisement.

Auto writer Eric Dahlquist was one of the first journalists to get behind the wheel of the Cobra Jet Mustang, and his praise was lavish. His report in the March 1968 issue of *Hot Rod* sounded an alarm for the competition and a celebration for the Ford faithful. "The Cobra Jet will be the utter delight of every Ford lover and the bane of all the rest because, quite frankly, it is the fastest running Pure Stock in the history of man." Prose like this couldn't come out of Ford's marketing machine, but coming from a magazine

From its functional hood scoop to the dual exhaust pipes, the 1968 Mustang Cobra Jet exuded subdued power. It garnered lavish press in the enthusiast's magazines of the day, prompting *Hot Rod* editor Eric Dahlquist to note, "The strength of a single Cobra Jet blast-off will put thousands into orbit for the nearest auto loan department."

The massive headers hanging under this 1968 Cobra Jet Mustang are not for show. They helped the 428-ci engine breathe on cue. The first fifty Cobra Jets came in Wimbledon White without a black hood stripe and had consecutive VINs.

like *Hot Rod* brought the customers into the showroom in droves. Dahlquist admitted in his article that ride and handling were marginal. A heavy engine in the nose combined with high-rate springs do nothing to smooth the ride. Though, he made it abundantly clear what the true purpose of the Cobra Jet was. "Whatever time is lost on turns, however, is immediately regained on the straightaway."

Because the GT model was mandatory to get the Cobra Jet engine option, grille

mounted road lamps were installed, as well as steel wheels, a "C" stripe on the side, and a narrow black hood paint stripe. Order the Cobra Jet engine with a four-speed tranny, and the dash held an 8,000-rpm tachometer. Each of the CJs had an "R" engine code as the fifth digit in the VIN number.

After the race cars were completed, regular production Cobra Jets started hitting the street, the option costing only $434. Transmission choices were two, a

(continued on page 58)

Cragar SS steel wheels were the standard hot rodder's replacement for factory units. All of the first fifty Cobra Jets were fastback models.

Modified for street competition, this 1968 Cobra Jet uses twin four-barrel carburetors to handle induction chores. The hood scoop covered the simple hole cut into the hood to allow cooler outside air to reach the engine.

Doing what it was built for, a 1968 Mustang Cobra Jet turns gasoline into long black stripes. Cobra Jets with a 4-speed manual transmission used staggered rear shocks to help control rear-axle hop under hard acceleration.

For 1968, Shelby started installing vents on the hood of the GT350 and GT500 for allowing excess heat to flow from the engine compartment. Superlative proportions were a Shelby Mustang hallmark in the first few years, as the numerous styling elements tended to work together.

Comfortable enough for long-distance travel, the 1968 GT350 was essentially a stock Mustang interior with additional improvements, such as the shoulder harnesses attached to the roll bar and the oil pressure and ammeter gauges in the center console.

Shelby tended to emphasize the long hood/short deck proportions of the Mustang fastback. The first year of Shelby Mustang production at the A.O. Smith Company plant in Livonia, Michigan, was 1968.

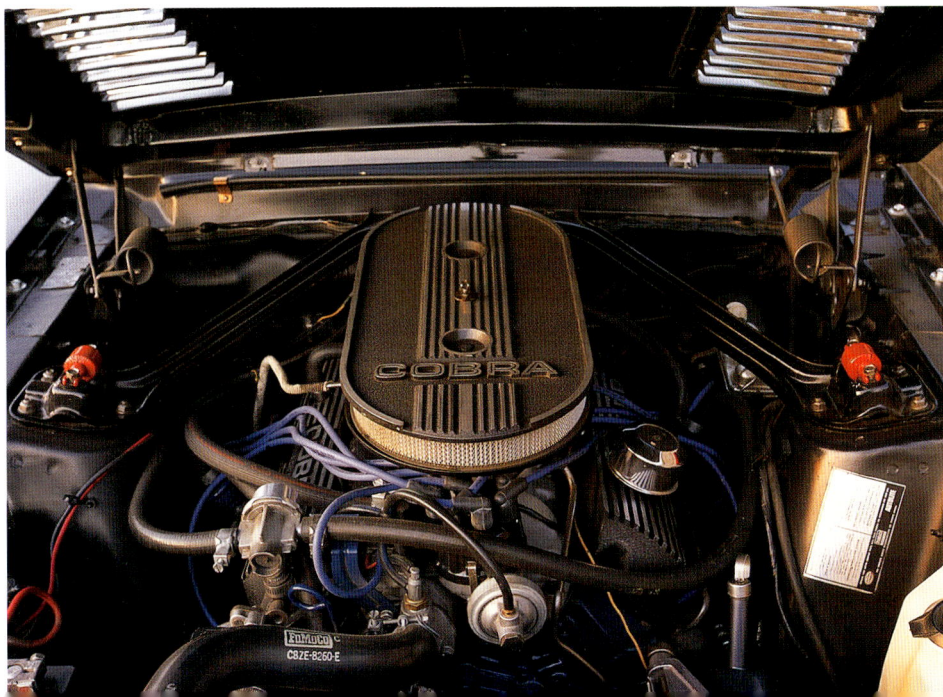

Both GT350 and GT500 Shelby Mustangs used the oval air cleaner housing in 1968. Under the long assembly was a single four-barrel carburetor on top of a 302-ci V-8, rated at 250 horsepower.

Introduced in the second half of the 1968 model run, the GT500KR was the top of the heap. Stuffing the Cobra Jet engine under the long fiberglass hood resulted in a strong quarter-mile run. Total production of the fastback version was 933 units.

strengthened 3-speed PGB-W C-6 automatic and the Top Loader manual 4-speed using an 11.5-inch single-plate dry clutch. The package was available only on GT models, but in all three body configurations: Fastback, coupe and convertible. While very few ragtops were built, 2,253 fastbacks were bought and 654 coupes found homes. Total Mustang production for 1968 was 317,148, and while Cobra Jet numbers were a drop in the bucket, its influence was far greater than its numbers would lead one to believe. It put the Mustang in the winner's column in a lot of NHRA events, and it shook up the competition for street supremacy. It proved that Ford was very serious about promoting brutal performance. And the best was yet to come.

1968 SHELBY GT500KR: WHEN IN DOUBT, GET A BIGGER STICK

Over the years, some people made the mistake of underestimating Carroll Shelby. This was usually done just once, and Shelby usually got the last laugh. Such was the case in the middle of the 1968 model year, when the GT500 was getting a little long in the tooth, at least in the world of muscle cars. A convertible was part of the model lineup for the first time in Shelby history and was popular with the public.

For 1968, the GT350 received a new engine, the Windsor 302-ci V-8. This iron block used a hydraulic camshaft and was topped with a single 4-barrel 600-cfm Holley carburetor. Output was listed at 250 horsepower, healthy enough but not the stuff of high-profile bench racing. But

drivers wanting to make a dramatic entrance looked to big brother. Other manufacturers were shoveling vast amounts of power under their hoods, and it wouldn't do to have the high-profile GT500 getting dusted by "lesser" makes. For 1968, the GT500 continued to employ the 428-ci, 360-horsepower engine that saw duty in 1967. In an effort to mainstream the vehicle, the multiple carburetors were yanked, replaced with a solitary 715-cfm Holley 4-barrel. This had no effect on power output. But halfway through the 1968s model run, an updated version of the GT500 hit the asphalt, equipped with the latest edition of a very big hammer . . . the Cobra Jet.

It was inevitable that the GT500 would get the newest high-performance mill that Ford had in the catalog.

Dearborn had no small amount of time and money invested in the Shelby, and to maintain bragging rights, more grunt was needed. The massive engine fit tightly in a standard Mustang, so it was a shoe-in for the Shelby. While the GT500 had plenty of tire-melting power, the Shelby was the living embodiment of "nothing succeeds like excess." With the demise of the Cobra sports car, the name Cobra was pressed into duty on the Shelby Mustang line. In the same vein of having too much, the mid-year revision of the GT500 was called the GT500KR, ostensibly for "King of the Road." Call it what ever you want, it was a beast.

Improvements to the GT500 were helpful in getting the power of the Cobra Jet translated into kinetic energy. Extra bracing around the front shock towers

No stranger to the drag strip, the 1968 GT500KR was laughably rated at 335 horsepower. It could cover the distance in 14.57 seconds at 99.56 miles per hour. For a vehicle tipping the scales at close to two tons, it was a feat.

The 1968 GT500KR used a Shelby-ized version of the Cobra Jet engine. A functional Ram Air induction system fed air through the twin scoops on the leading edge of the hood directly into the air cleaner. For the first time, the hood was held shut with the installation of Dzus twist-type hood locks, replacing the pin-on-a-cable system used in prior years.

handled the torque and stiffened the front suspension. At the other end, the rear shocks were staggered in 4-speed equipped cars to help dampen the inevitable spring wind-up during hard acceleration. The Traction-Lok rear end was standard on KRs, 3.25:1 on C-6 automatic transmission equipped cars, 3.50:1 gears if a Top-Loader, big input, close-ratio 4-speed manual was installed. The C-6 tranny used a cast-iron tail shaft for strength. Buyers who wanted the optional 4.11 or 4.33 gearset found the differential filled with the factory installed Detroit Locker. To help slow the hard-running Shelbys were wider rear brake shoes and drums (1.75 inches), as well as upgraded wheel cylinders. Customers checking the order form for air

conditioning found an engine oil cooler under the ram-air hood.

As detailed elsewhere in this chapter, all 428s are not created equal. In the KR, it was essentially a 428-ci iron block fitted with a pair of low-riser heads from the famed 427-ci racing engine, and it was rated at a laughable 335 horsepower at 5,200 rpm. It put out far more, and the results were borne out on the drag strip. In the October 1968 issue of *Car Life*, a Fastback version was flogged. The big guy ran down the quarter-mile in only 14.57 seconds at 99.56 miles per hour. Acceleration from 0 to 60 miles per hour took only 6.5 seconds. These are impressive numbers, especially when you consider the grade of tires during that era. Fifteen-inch Goodyear E70 Polyglas tires can handle only so much rotational energy. Push the accelerator too far into the carpet and wheelspin quickly factored into the equation. But with the massive torque available in the low and mid-range, a GT500KR could effortlessly lope along all day.

With the sizable lump of iron over the front wheels, handling was not quite in the same league as the lighter GT350 and nowhere near what Shelby GT350s were like even two years before. Spring rates were sizeable, with 360-lb/in coils in the front, 135-lb/in 4-leaf semi-elliptic springs at the back. Shelby ads of the day push the fact that the GT500KR held a "drag champion engine." Whereas the 1966 model was a thinly disguised road-racing car, the 1968 GT500KR was a street stormer, able to hold its own between stoplights on a Saturday night. The rest of the week, it could behave like a mainstream vehicle. Kind of like having your cake and eating it too.

For the first time, the 428 emblem graced the fender of a Shelby Mustang with the 1968 GT500KR. The KR designation stood for "King of the Road," a slick marketing move by the master of automotive marketing, Carroll Shelby. His cars could walk the walk.

With genuine simulated woodgrain inserts on the dash, the upscale aura of the GT500KR was visible. Comfortably appointed, a Shelby Mustang was a Grand Touring car in the European tradition. No surprise, as Carroll Shelby had spent a considerable amount of time on the Continent during his days as a winning race driver.

Contrasting C-stripes were part of the GT Package, as well as a heavy-duty suspension, dual exhaust, GT emblems on the front fenders and a GT-labeled gas cap.

The addition of aftermarket traction bars attest to this 1968 Mustang GTs owner's desire for improved grip off the line. Smoother side scoops are the quickest way to differentiate this Mustang from a 1967.

As used in the Steve McQueen movie *Bullitt,* a 1968 Mustang GT equipped with a 390-ci engine set the standard for movie car chases. For the film, the Mustang emblem in the grill was removed.

CHAPTER 3
THE STORM BEFORE THE CALM

When an earthquake happens on the floor of the Pacific Ocean, it can generate tidal waves of frightful proportions called tsunamis. They can slip through the ocean for thousands of miles with virtually no visible trace on the surface, undetected. But as they close on a shoreline, the energy is released.

A wall of fast-moving water grows in size until it crashes down on the unsuspecting landmass. Much the same phenomena was about to take place all over America, as the horsepower race between auto manufacturers grew to truly crazy proportions. The pure race cars of only a handful of years earlier couldn't hold a candle to the street legal vehicles that anyone with a driver's license could point down Woodward Avenue.

The Performance War was heating up to a white-hot intensity. And leading the wave of power was the Mustang, an earthquake that affected the entire automotive landscape. When it receded, nothing would be the same.

The 1970 Boss 302 enjoyed 56/44 front/rear weight distribution in its pursuit of a competitive edge. Both front and rear fender lips had to be rolled to allow clearance for the F60x15 tires.

A rarely seen model is the 1969 Mustang GT convertible. The GT Package was a $146.71 option and was quickly eclipsed by the Mach 1. Like earlier years, GTs were equipped with the Competition Suspension, dual exhaust, and lower body stripes.

1969 MUSTANG GT: INADVERTENT COMPETITION

In the world of muscle car engines, size does matter. One of the Ten Commandments of Horsepower states, "There is NO Substitute for Cubic Inches." Financial considerations dictated that casting a big-displacement block, filling it with hardy mechanicals, and dropping it into a mid-sized vehicle was far more cost-effective than installing a high-tech, high-dollar, high-revving small-block. Every muscle car maker had grasped this essential truth, as had the legion of buyers that wanted a fast, cheap, good-looking ride, the faster and cheaper the better. Ford had been caught asleep at the switch when the

original Mustang debuted, though few could have seen the need to install a big-block engine into an automobile so small. In just a couple of years, the public was clamoring for larger engines. The engine compartments of the early Mustangs just weren't roomy enough to handle anything bigger than the 289-ci power-plant. When the 390-ci engine was shoehorned in for the 1967 model year, some compromises had to be faced. There was virtually zero room between the shock towers and the cylinder heads. Larger engines were on their way, and there was no way Ford was letting the Mustang miss out on them.

Word came from on high that the 1969 Mustang must be able to swallow any and all engines in the Ford roster, present and future. That meant that the rest of the vehicle would need to be enlarged to maintain the proper proportions. The wheelbase was unchanged, but after that, all bets were off. Overall length was increased, primarily due to the pronounced front overhang. Interior room was enlarged, with two inches of additional shoulder room and one inch of hip room through the use of thinner doors. When the 1969 Mustang lineup was released, the lineage was unmistakable, yet the design was more muscular. It looked fast just sitting in a driveway, but Ford made sure its performance could back up the visuals.

As in years past, three body styles were offered, but the nomenclature had changed. While the convertible was still called a convertible, the coupe was now called a hardtop. And what had been the fastback was now called the SportsRoof. Under the sleek new skin was basically the same mechanical setup that had been under the 1968 model. That included the short/long-arm front independent suspension, a Hotchkiss live rear axle, recirculating ball steering, and a 38-foot turning circle. New editions were slipped into the Mustang roster, but one option package was still available that had been around since the 'Stang was first introduced—the GT. Compared to some of the other types of Mustangs in the 1969 menu, the GT almost looked understated. It was the ideal sleeper Mustang.

The $147 1969 GT Equipment Group took its styling cues from preceding years, which meant rocker panel stripes, argent-colored steel wheels with GT logos on the wheel covers, and a Competition Suspension. Pin-type hood latches (à la NASCAR) was a boy-racer touch, as was the nonfunctional hood scoop with integrated turn-signal indicators. Drum brakes on all four corners, dual exhaust, and a 3-speed manual transmission rounded out the GT Package. It was not possible to order the GT option with a six-cylinder engine or the 302-ci mill. But the choices of engines that could be fitted were anything but pretend.

The standard power plant was a 351-ci V8, dubbed the "Windsor" due to its Windsor, Ontario origins. It was essentially a stroked 302-ci engine. Bore and stroke came in at 4.00x3.5 inches, and the 1-inch raised deck height helped in generating good low- and mid-range torque. With 9.5:1 compression and using a Motorcraft 350-cfm two-barrel carburetor, it generated 250 horsepower at 4,600 rpm with parallel valves set in a wedge combustion chamber. The Windsor was a tough, understressed power plant that would prove to be popular with shade-tree mechanics.

A graceful design, the 1969 Mustang GT convertible was a wonderful way to soak in the sounds and smell of the ocean on a summer day. Triple vertical taillights in a concave panel were exclusive to the 1969 models.

However, the GT package allowed a buyer to peruse the engine option list with glee. The next engine on the performance ladder was a 290-horsepower version of the 351W. This was accomplished by dropping a 470-cfm 4-barrel carburetor on the intake manifold. Need more ponies? The trusty 390-ci engine was still being offered, but the end of its road was in sight. Rated at 320 horsepower, it used a 470-cfm Autolite carb and made good torque, but the additional weight negated the extra power. Handling was adversely affected as well, and Mustangs with this option preferred to go straight. At the top of the power list was the massive 428 Cobra Jet, introduced in 1968. With 335 advertised horsepower, this engine was covered extensively in the preceding chapter. It had not changed since its 1968 debut. But in the 1969 GTs equipped with 428 Cobra Jets, the faux hood scoop was ditched in favor of a "Shaker" scoop, so named because the entire scoop/air cleaner assembly projected out of a large hole cut in the middle of the hood. With heavy throttle, the cast alloy scoop shook with the rest of the engine. It made for a great show.

Unfortunately for the GT, it ended up getting little promotion in the showroom, and Ford had a model of Mustang debuting in 1969 that would overshadow the GT in a big way. The Mach 1 was a high-profile boulevard bruiser that was the rolling epitome of "Flash," and the public flocked to the showroom. Sales for the GT were low, very low. So it was with little fanfare that Ford pulled the plug on the GT option package. In all three body styles, the GT only amassed 5,396 sales, which translates to rarity today. While not as visually striking as some of the

1969 Mach 1s used a plaque on the nonfunctional hood scoop to denote engine displacement. This was the only year that the Mustang used a quad headlight setup.

other model Mustangs in 1969, the properly optioned GT could hold its own with most 'Stangs.

1969 MACH 1: SOUNDS LIKE SERIOUS VELOCITY

New on the Mustang scene was a model that reflected the times perfectly: the Mach 1. Bold, vivid, the fashions of the day saw their automotive equivalent with the muscle cars. All of the manufacturers were building vehicles that vied for

attention through the use of bright colors, big engines, or a combination of the two. Ford unleashed a bevy of high-profile Mustangs for 1969, going head-to-head with the Camaro/Firebird, Barracuda, and others the Blue Oval knew were coming from the competition.

In the March 1969 issue of *Car Life*, they started off with a question: "Are you ready for the first great Mustang? One with performance to match its looks, handling to send imported-car fans home mumbling to themselves, and an interior as elegant and livable as a gentleman's club?"

Right off the bat, it was clear that the Mach 1 targeted buyers that didn't mind being seen. This was not the vehicle in which a shrinking violet would roll past. From its race car hood pins to the rear lip spoiler, the Mach 1 could be tailored from mild to wild with the stroke of a pen. Engine options ranged from strong to brutal. Available only on the SportsRoof

The hood was painted a low-gloss black, similar to the finish used on top of a P-51 Mustang engine cowling. The large, sloping rear window was a strong stylistic element, but it compromised headroom in the already tight rear seats.

A reflective stripe wrapped around the tail of the 1969 Mach 1, following the line set by the bumper. This 390-ci example sports the standard Mach 1 chrome-styled steel wheels with E70x14 tires.

model, the Mach 1 eclipsed the GT model's sales in short order, selling 72,458 in 1969. That kind of popularity was due to the fact that the Mach 1 could be whatever the buyer wanted, from a comfortable long-distance Grand Tourer to a quarter-mile warrior. Adding $508 to the price of a $2,618 regular SportsRoof model brought the starting price of a Mach 1 to $3,126, a relative bargain considering the performance potential.

One of the first things anyone noticed about the Mach 1 was the low-gloss blacked-out hood. This, along with the reflective side stripe, was a styling motif that Ford put to good use. Like the GT, the Mach 1 came with the standard 250-horsepower 351W V-8 engine, topped with a two-barrel carburetor atop a cast-iron intake manifold, and optional engines included the 290-horsepower

351W, 320-horsepower 390-ci, and the 335-horsepower 428 Cobra Jet. This broad line-up allowed customers to buy as much engine as they wanted and could afford. The option list was as long as your arm and full of high-performance good buys. Stepping up to the 290-horsepower small block only cost $26 in the Mach 1. If you wanted a big block but didn't need the Cobra Jet, the 320-horsepower, 390-ci engine only cost $100. If a buyer wanted the Cobra Jet, one had to fatten the check by only $224. For the Ram Air Cobra Jet, the option price was $357. This engine setup was new for 1969, and with its Shaker hood, it injected even more power into an engine that wasn't suffering from any surfeit of grunt. The optional Ram Air package used a vacuum diaphragm–operated flap that would

(continued on page 74)

The Deluxe Interior was standard on the Mach 1, including high-back seats, Rim-Blow steering wheel, and wood-grained appliqué. The functional Shaker hood scoop loomed in front of the driver, vibrating in time with the engine.

With a 428 Cobra Jet engine under the hood, this 1969 Mach 1 could hold its own on a Saturday night. Faux scoops were fitted under the rear quarter windows on all SportsRoofs, with the exception of the Boss 302 in 1969, in an effort to capture some of the racer image that Shelby products had in spades.

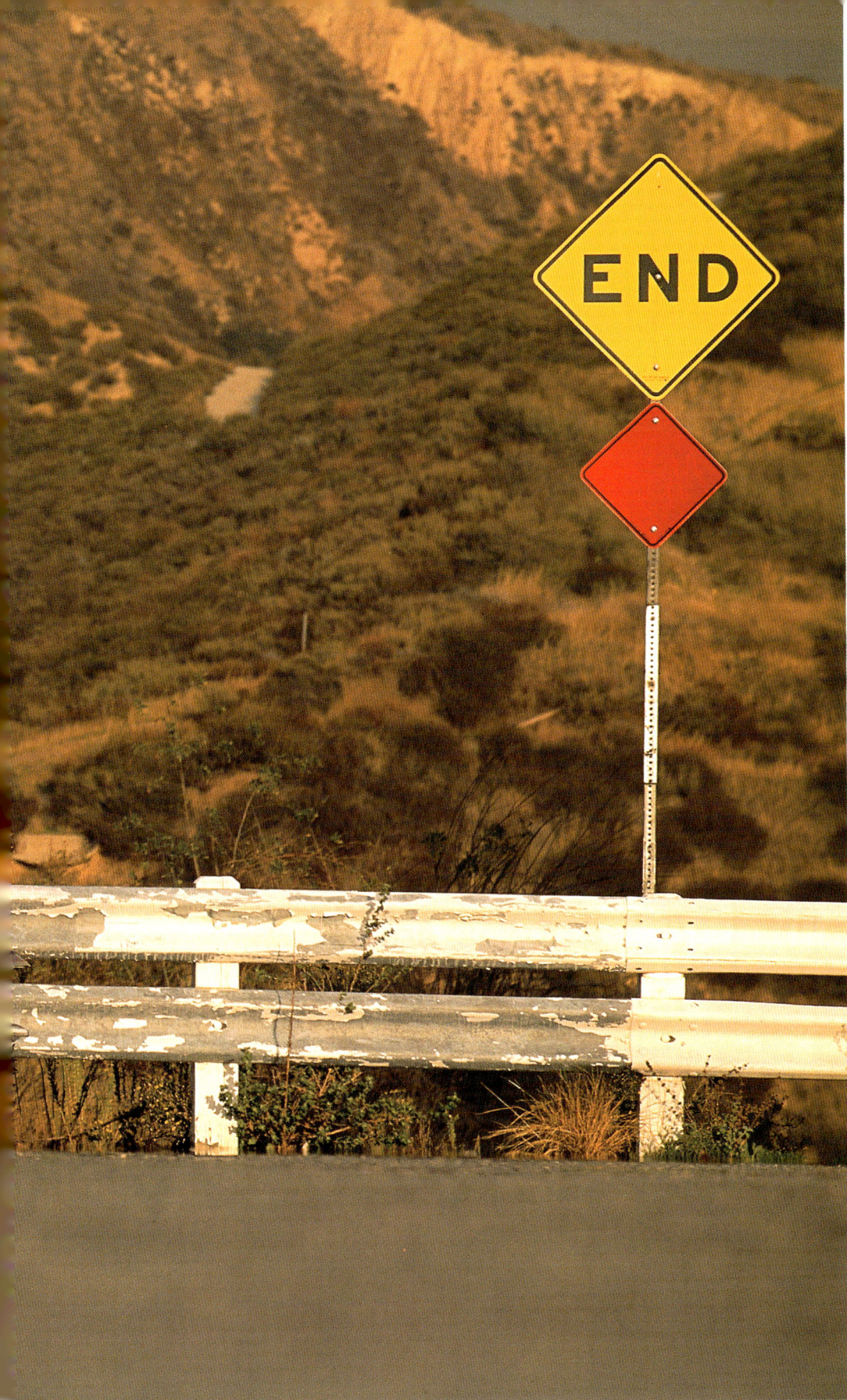

Debuting in the 1969 model year, the Mach 1 quickly became the favorite of buyers wanting a sporting Mustang that looked the part. The Mach 1 was only available with the SportsRoof body style and used plenty of graphic elements to attract the eye. The horizontal stripe in the center of the door was made of reflecting tape.

allow cool ambient air to enter the air cleaner under heavy throttle. Officially, Ford listed the output of a Ram Air equipped engine the same as a regular Cobra Jet at 335 horsepower. With the regular Cobra Jet making close to 400 horsepower, the infusion of cool air only boosted the formidable engine's output. On the quarter-mile, it was usually good for a tenth of a second. Ducking the scrutiny of the insurance industry was hard work.

Underpinnings were identical to the low-visibility GT package. The Competition Suspension was standard on the Mach 1, and it was made of beefier springs and shock absorbers, as well as a large .95-inch front anti-roll bar. On vehicles with the 428 Cobra Jet engine and a 4-speed manual transmission, staggered rear shocks were installed to help control wheel hop. Front coil springs were rated at 123 lb/in, while the rear semi-elliptical leaf springs came in at 140 lb/in. Steering was of the affordable recirculating ball gear design with a ratio of 20.3:1, giving the Mach 1 a turning circle of 38 feet. The steering needed four turns lock-to-lock, handy when parking a big-block engined example bereft of optional power steering, but on a twisty road the driver's arms would flail about madly. Most customers felt that the most important control was the accelerator pedal.

The 1969 Mach 1 made a big splash in the automotive press of the day. In the

The 1969 Mach 1 was the first muscle car to sport a Shaker hood scoop, which bolted directly to the air cleaner assembly. As the engine was revved, the scoop moved as the engine rocked on its mounts. It did little for performance but looked great.

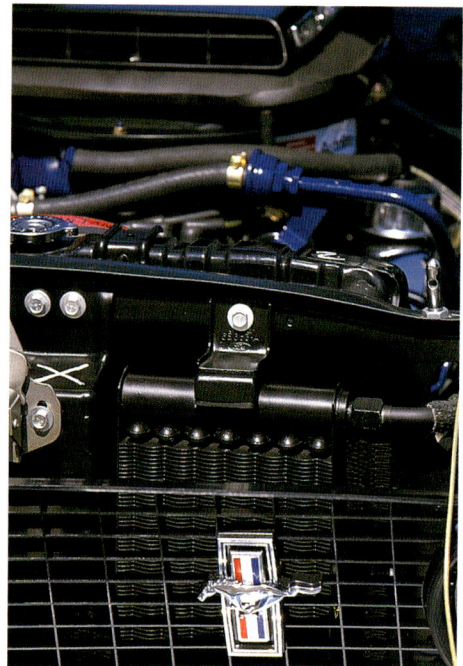

Mach 1s equipped with the Super Cobra Jet option used an oil cooler mounted ahead of the radiator support. On vehicles equipped with a Shaker hood scoop, a rubber skirt fit against the inside of the hood around the hole cut out for the scoop. A drain hose let rain and wash water flow away from the engine.

March 1969 issue of *Car Life*, their testers ran a battery of tests on a 428 Cobra Jet equipped beast and found that cracking the 14-second quarter-mile was child's play. The aggressively-styled Mustang delivered a 13.90 run at 103.32 miles per hour. As each horse had to haul just 11.1 pounds of car, and it was fitted with a 3.50:1 limited-slip axle ratio, top speed came in at 121 miles per hour. Just what was needed for a quick trip to the grocery store.

Customers who ordered either the 3.91:1 Traction-Lok or the 4.30:1 Detroit Locker rear axle ratio found that they now owned a Super Cobra Jet. Made expressly to lunge down the drag strip, this $6.53 option has to be one of the greatest deals in muscle cardom, as it filled the engine with performance parts Ford developed for motorsports. Though Cobra Jet engines, both regular and Super, were fitted with two-bolt main bearing caps, Ford engineered their durability. With C8AE-numbered connecting rods from the Ford GT MkIV LeMans 427-ci engine used cap screws and 7/16-inch rod bolts, stretching of the con rods under high-rpm conditions was not an issue. Attached to the top of the rods were special forged aluminum pistons. The change from a standard Cobra Jet's reciprocating mass required rebalancing the engine as well as an external counterbalancer. Also visible under the hood was the engine oil cooler bolted onto the radiator support.

Two transmissions were offered, the C-6 3-speed automatic transmission and a top-loader 4-speed manual. At the other

A graceful C-pillar formed the basis for the SportsRoof body type, the only style the 1969 Mach 1 was available in. Being a 428 Super Cobra Jet, this Mach 1 was equipped with either a 3.91:1 or 4.30:1 rear axle ratio.

Optional rear window slats and rear wing added attitude to this already healthy 1969 428 Cobra Jet Mach 1. The pop-open gas cap was part of the standard Mach 1 package, as was the dual exhaust with chrome quad extensions. The rumble that flowed from them tended to get attention.

end of the driveshaft was an N-case nodular iron, 9-inch differential, known for its bulletproof longevity, as well as a pair of massive 31-spline axles. The tires of the day, Goodyear Polyglas GT F70-14s, were the best on the market, but were no match for the tremendous torque. Driving in wet conditions was a quick way to raise the heart rate.

The Mach 1's interior came in one configuration—Deluxe. High-back front bucket seats, replete with Comfortweave knitted-vinyl inserts, a Rim-Blow steering wheel, center console, genuine simulated teakwood-grained trim, a clock, and 55 extra pounds of sound insulation were standard on the Mach 1. The huge C-pillar caused a bit of a blind spot, but a squeeze of the accelerator tended to make other vehicles recede in the mirrors. For long-distance trips, the Mach 1 was a comfortable two-person car. With a trunk of only 5 cubic-feet capacity, the backseat came in handy for suitcases. The image most buyers wanted to project was of an unbridled beast of a car. Depending on the options chosen, the Mach 1 could live up to the promise. If a customer

Built to turn as well as it accelerated and braked, the 1969 Boss 302 was designed to be able to out-handle any comparable vehicle. Wheels such as these were popular aftermarket purchases, making the standard Magnum 500 15x7 wheels especially valuable.

wanted to be the boss of the street, well, Ford had a car for them as well.

1969 BOSSES: 302 & 429 SUSPENDING BELIEF

To say that a Mustang buyer had options was a gross understatement. The order form listed the base Mustang, the GT, and the Mach 1. As if that wasn't enough, Ford wanted to go racing—badly. The company had recently hired away from General Motors a race-loving manager, Bunkie Knudsen, who consistently transformed staid GM divisions into competition-beating dynamos. When the GM presidency went to Ed Cole, Knudsen came into the Blue Oval's fold in February 1968 as the 1969 Mustangs were well on their way to production. But he brought along a talented designer, Larry Shinoda, who had an impressive portfolio. The seminal 1963 split-window Corvette Sting Ray was one of his projects, as were both Mako Sharks. He showed his skill in enhancing an automobile's image when he conceived of the Z28 Camaro. In fact that vehicle guided his first project for

Larry Shinoda designed the C-stripe that graced the side of the 1969 Boss 302, as well as the blacked-out headlight coves and hood. Unlike most of the 1969 Mustang line, a hood scoop was not available on the Boss 302.

Ford, a direct competitor to Chevrolet. Borrowing from the street slang for cool, he forwarded "Boss" to the powers-that-be in Dearborn. At first, they had a difficult time understanding it, but they soon approved the vehicles that would become the Boss 302 and the Boss 429—two different Mustangs for two different purposes.

Chevrolet knew that selling a car was easier with racing in its background. The Camaro Z28 was aimed at the SCCA Trans-Am racing series, and the combination of a high-revving small-block engine in a taut, good-handling chassis put the Bow Tie in the winner's circle. With the Blue Oval firm seeing the publicity that Chevrolet was garnering with the Z28, they felt it was imperative that the Mustang battle, fender-to-fender, on the

track. However, SCCA homologation rules required that Ford build at least 1,000 street examples of the model with which they wanted to compete.

As Mike Mueller recounts in his book *Mustang,* Ford wanted some of that action. So Knudsen decreed that his engineers produce "absolutely the best-handling street car on the American market."

Working with Kar Kraft Engineering in Brighton, Michigan, the first of these prototypes was assembled in just three weeks. This was the start of the Boss 302. Further development of the car then went to Ford Engineering.

Starting with a SportsRoof model, the Dearborn-built 1969 Boss 302 was trimmed and tweaked to perfection. The engine at the heart of the Boss 302

was the result of power-loving engineers with the freedom to experiment. Deep in the bowels of Ford Engineering, a new 351-ci engine was being developed for use in the 1970 lineup. Though this new engine and the 351-Windsor shared the same displacement, similarities ended there. Dubbed "the Cleveland," due to the location of the foundry, it was blessed with a set of cylinder heads that drew heavily on racing experience. These heads boasted canted valves that used as straight an induction path as possible to generate maximum flow. To that goal, Ford installed huge valves, 2.24-inch intake and 1.71-inch exhaust.

Fitting a pair of these heads on one of the Tunnel-Port 302-ci racing engines from the 1968 season, the engineers saw immediate results. The Performance Engine Group found that starting with a race engine had its advantages. Designing the power plant for a racing environment, then tuning it down for street use, resulted in a tough, affordable engine that Ford could then use to qualify the race engine for Trans-Am work. And that's exactly what happened.

A street Boss 302 mill was not an engine for the neophyte. With a cross-drilled forged-steel crankshaft, forged connecting rods, 10.6:1 compression, and solid valve lifters, it wasn't the type of engine that thrived on marginal maintenance. It needed premium fuel and lots of it. With a Holley R-4511 four-barrel carburetor flowing 780 cfm, the 20-gallon gas tank needed frequent visits to Sunoco. The carb sat on a cast aluminum high-rise intake manifold that was

A road race car with a license plate, the 1969 Boss 302 was built to satisfy the SCCA to allow the car to compete in Trans-Am racing. Designer Larry Shinoda insisted that the scoop installed on the side of the standard SportsRoof body be deleted on the Boss 302.

Understated to a fault, Ford poured large sums of money into the mechanicals of the 1969 Boss 429. Production was low, with only 857 of these built in the first half of 1969, while 499 1970 models were assembled in the late summer of 1969.

designed to maximize upper-rpm response. So fast would the Boss 302 engine collect revolutions, that the factory installed a rev limiter in an attempt to reduce the chance of owners spinning the power plant into an early grave. In order to stay low on the insurance industry's radar screen, Ford took the opposite tack in rating the Boss 302, stating that the potent small-block cranked out 290 horsepower and 290 lb/ft of torque. In reality, those were very healthy horses indeed. Anthony Young writes in his book *Ford Hi-Po V-8 Muscle*

Cars, that Ford engineer William Barr recalled that the 1969 Boss 302 "had the same power rating as the Z-28: 290 horsepower and 290 lb/ft of torque. In fact, the average power of ten production Boss 302 engines was something like 314 horsepower on a 'B' curve (with the engine fully equipped as it would leave the engine plant). On an 'A' curve (the engineering maximum power test without air cleaner but with dynamometer exhaust headers), it went over 390 horsepower. The street vehicle exhaust system was designed with about a 2 $\frac{1}{2}$

inch Hg restriction so that the Boss 302 developed over 300 horsepower as installed in the vehicle."

Better yet, Ford succeeded in fulfilling Bunkie Knudsen's edict to build the best-handling vehicle on the road. The suspension was labeled "competition-type" in Ford's literature, and in 1969 that meant firm. Spring rates were substantial, the front coils measuring 350 lb/in and the 4-leaf rear springs coming in at 150 lb/in. Gabriel made the shock absorbers, which had a 1.1875-inch piston diameter. The rear shocks were

staggered to dampen axle hop during hard acceleration, the left shock positioned to the rear of the axle, while the right side Gabriel was mounted in front of it. Speaking of the solid rear axle, it was filled with a semi-floating, straddle-mounted pinion with a heavy-duty 9-inch ring gear and 31-spline axle shafts. The standard axle ratio in the 1969 Boss 302 was 3.50:1, with a trio of optional gearsets: 3.50:1, 3.91:1, and 4.30:1 Traction-Lok. A link-type stabilizer bar was fitted at the front, .85 inches in diameter and made of SAE 1090 steel.

Surprisingly low-key for such a potent package, the 1969 Boss 429 existed to allow Ford to race the monster engine in NASCAR. The only visual indications of its powerplant were the small decals on the front fenders, a chin spoiler slightly smaller than the Boss 302's, and the huge functional hood scoop.

The monochromatic paint scheme was an attempt by Ford to hold down costs of the 1969 Boss 429. Goodyear F70x15 tires were standard on the Boss 429, though they stood little chance of handling the 450 lb-ft of torque at 3,400 rpm.

Steering response was quickened from the stock Mustang with the fitting of a 16:1 fast-ratio steering box, improving the nimbleness of the pony car on a winding road.

But properly driven, the 1969 Boss 302 would exercise the speedometer with abandon. In their June 1969 issue, *Car and Driver* magazine ran an example on the drag strip, covering the quarter-mile in 14.57 seconds at 97.57 miles per hour. With a 0 to 60 time of 6 seconds, and 100 miles per hour showing on the speedo in 15.2 seconds from rest, the Boss 302 didn't need to make any apologies. Only 1,628 Boss 302s were built for 1969, making them relatively rare.

Yours truly owned one in the 1970s,

and the feeling that I was behind the wheel of a missile was reinforced every time I mashed the accelerator into the carpet and the small-block came on cam. Bucking and snorting at a light, it was only happy when the tachometer needle was heading north of 3,000 rpm. Gawd, it was fun.

WHEN IN DOUBT, GET A BIGGER STICK

Not every racetrack was ideal for the Boss 302 engine. At the same time, Ford needed to homologate the massive 429-ci engine for use in NASCAR. The 426 Hemis from Chrysler had handed Ford its lunch in the mid-1960s, and to right that wrong, the engineers in Dearborn were tasked with designing an engine that could meet, and hopefully beat, the dominant Hemis. Bunkie Knudsen had just taken the helm at Ford, and he wanted the newest and strongest engine installed in the Mustang. What Bunkie wanted, he generally got, and what Ford came up with was the stuff of legend.

Rather than build an all-new engine, Ford started with a big-block engine already in the inventory but heavily massaged it. Using the "385" family of engines that debuted in 1968, the new mill displaced 429 ci, later growing to 460 to coax Lincolns and Thunderbirds down the road. The cast-iron block was a beefy component with short skirts to allow future displacement increases. But what set the Boss 429 engine apart from its docile sedan counterparts were its aluminum heads.

Realizing that the best way to develop power would be to move as much fuel/air mixture through the engine as quickly as possible, the engine designers knew the flow benefits of a hemispherical combustion chamber. Using canted valves and a centrally located spark plug, such a design would improve flame propagation in the cylinder and provide faster ingress and egress of gases. It worked for Chrysler, and it was hoped that it would work for Ford, especially on the banked tracks of NASCAR. What the engineers came up with would be known as the "Blue Crescent 429," or "twisted Hemi," referring to the splayed configuration of the valve train under the huge valve covers. In its final production version, the spark-plugs were positioned to one side of the combustion chamber, resulting in something of a "semi-Hemi" layout.

In order to generate the big numbers needed for victory on the track, big

The hood scoop on the Boss 429 was opened and shut via cable to a knob under the dash that the driver could operate at will. It was to be opened during periods of heavy throttle and shut when the engine was cold, allowing the powerplant to warm up.

Early 1969 Boss 429 production used "S" code engines filled with NASCAR-grade connecting rods and Cobra Jet hydraulic camshafts. They were topped with magnesium valve covers but changed to cast aluminum with the 280th Boss 429 built.

Like the 1969 Boss 302, the 1970 edition had a trunk lid painted in low-gloss black paint. The taillight treatment differed from 1969, as the 1970 model used a flat panel between the recessed lights. Rear window slats and a spoiler were options.

valves were used. The intake valves measured 2.275 inches in diameter, while the exhaust valves came in at 1.895 inches. Special chrome-molly/cobalt-steel alloy valve seat inserts were shrink-fit into the aluminum heads, permanently bonding them. Aiding in gas flow were huge circular ports, matched to the high-rise intake manifold. Perched on top was a 735-cfm Holley 4-barrel carburetor, sucking cool ambient air when the driver manually opened the functional hood scoop's hungry maw. A dual-point, dual-advance distributor was used, with Autolite AF-32 spark plugs used to fire the mixture.

Other standard goodies included a high-capacity oil cooler, power steering with an oil cooler, special high-performance suspension, including front and rear stabilizer bars, and a "Traction-Lok" rear axle with a 3.91:1 ratio. Optional gearsets for the pumpkin ranged from 3.50:1 to a stump-pulling 4.30:1.

In order to run on the track, it had to be available on the street. After a Mustang SportsRoof was identified as a Boss 429 vehicle rolling down the assembly line, it was fitted with the standard and mandatory options needed but no engine. Ford's race shop, Kar Kraft, shoe-horned the monster engine into the Mustang, as well as massaging other critical areas. Clearance between the heads and the shock towers was a concern solved by essentially cutting the stock towers away and building custom components. Beefy bracing connecting the

towers to the firewall was fitted to keep cowl-shake to a minimum. The battery was installed in the trunk, partly to help offset the heavy engine over the front wheels, and partly due to a lack of space under the hood.

Ford rated the hydraulic camshaft "S" code engine at 375 horsepower at 5,200 rpm, with torque queuing up at 450 lb/ft at 3,400. Later "T" code engines used mechanical camshafts and were rated at 25 horsepower more. These numbers didn't fool anyone. While the rev limiter, smallish carburetor, and restrictive exhaust did nothing for output, by removing or replacing them, power levels rose to startling heights. In stock form, the Boss 429 roared from 0 to 60 miles per hour in 7.1 seconds for the July 1969

issue of *Car Life*, handling the quarter-mile in 14.09 seconds at 102.85 miles per hour. A well-driven Mach 1 would walk away from the Boss 429. But when the lads at *Car Life* made a couple of modifications under the hood, the top Boss roared down the drag strip in 12.32 seconds at 113.49 miles per hour. Considering that the power had to flow through F60x15 Super Wide Oval Fiberglass belted tires, these numbers give a strong indication of the rotational energy the race-based engine made.

If it's rarity you seek, then the Boss 429 should be on your list. Only 857 units were built between January and July 1969. Each one was basically a hand-built street-able race car. Never an inexpensive car (the Boss 429 engine

The cast alloy Shaker hood scoop was a $65 option on the 1970 Boss 302, allowing cool air to be directed into the air cleaner.

alone listed at $1,208 on the invoice Ford sent to Kar Kraft), first and foremost it was meant to compete in motorsports. That a version actually made it onto the streets and into the hands of the public is a feat that must be credited to Bunkie Knudsen.

replaced with a flat insert and flanked by recessed lights. The simulated air scoops under the quarter panels were a styling element that Larry Shinoda had balked against in the 1969 Mustangs. He was able to get the Boss 302 released without the scoop, but not the Mach 1 and Boss

The Boss 302 engine was slightly different in 1970 than the preceding year. Intake valves were reduced in size to 2.19 inches to improve the engine's street manners. The crankshaft was switched to a non-cross-drilled item in 1970.

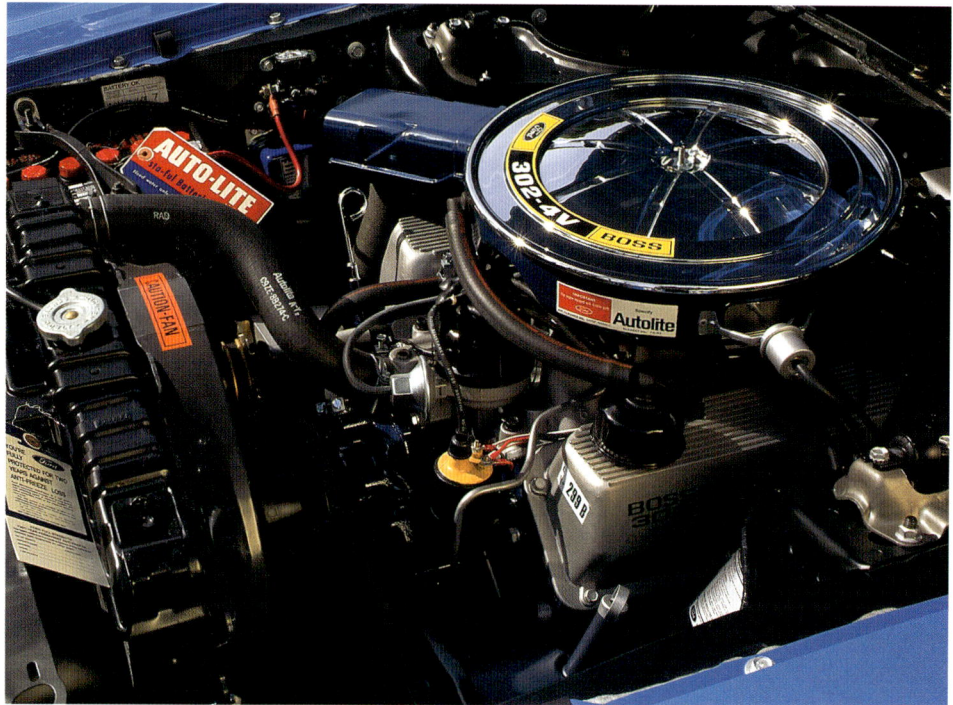

SECOND VERSE, DIFFERENT THAN THE FIRST

Round two came in 1970, as the second year of the Boss 302 and Boss 429 saw the headlight treatment for the entire Mustang line carry over to the street-able racers. A different hood treatment and side stripe on the Boss 302, as well as the black finished hood scoop on Boss 429s, were strong graphic touches. The 1969 model's outboard headlights were replaced with faux vents, turning the Mustang into a two-headlight vehicle again. The taillight treatment changed as well, with the 1969's concave panel

429. In order to visually differentiate the 1969 and 1970 models, the scoop was eliminated completely for 1970. The result was a clean shoulder line, kicking up aft of the door. Like the 1969 Boss 302, the front fenders had been rolled outward for tire clearance.

The Boss 302 had changes deeper than sheet metal. Ford engineers had hoped to install a rear anti-sway bar on the 1969 model, but didn't get that chance. For 1970, a rear bar was installed measuring $5/8$ inches in diameter, while the front bar was fattened up to $15/16$ inch. In 1969, the dual exhaust system had both cylinder banks dumping gases into a single, transverse muffler, and venting via dual tips. For 1970, each exhaust pipe had its own muffler. Compression stayed the same as in 1969 at 10.5:1, and carburetion was still a large single Holley 4-barrel.

At the other end of the vehicle, the engine was mildly revised, with the 2.24-inch diameter intake valves found on the 1969 Boss 302 replaced with 2.19-inch units in an effort to increase lower-rpm response. Exhaust valves stayed the same 1.717-inch diameter. Some owners had complained that the 1969 Boss 302's engine needed to be revved too highly for their liking in order to extract its power. Besides the valves being changed, the chrome valve covers used in 1969 were replaced with cast aluminum pieces. A significant difference between the two years was the replacement of the 1969 Boss 302's cross-drilled crankshaft with a non-cross-drilled affair. For the first time, Boss 302s could be ordered with a functional Shaker Ram Air hood scoop. This was an option for 1970, though it's a rare sight to see a 1970 Boss 302 without it today. Another seldom-seen item on 1970 Boss 302s were the standard "dog-dish" hubcaps and trim rings. Magnum 500 wheels dipped in chrome were an option, and today they seem the norm. The sizable rear spoiler had been made of plastic for 1969 and was found to warp. To correct the problem for 1970, the wing was constructed of fiberglass. It cured the warping problem, but the additional weight was too much for the trunk-lid springs. In response to the trunk not staying open, Ford installed a prop rod. Problem fixed.

Inside, the low-backed seats of 1969 were replaced with high-backed thrones for 1970. The manual transmission shifter was a standard Ford affair in the first year of Boss 302 production, but in the 1970 models a Hurst Competition Plus T-handle came standard. Otherwise, the driver faced the same 8,000-rpm tachometer, the same 120 mile-per-hour

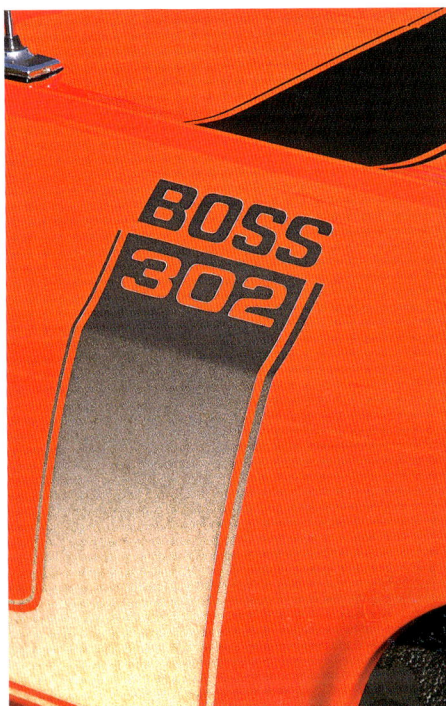

Reflective tape on the front fenders of the 1970 Boss 302 glowed at night when struck with headlights.

speedometer, and the same rapidly falling fuel gauge. Firm pressure on the accelerator brought a torrent of acceleration as the engine wound up, the solid lifter valve train chattered madly, and the exhaust gases found their way aft. The blend of sensations was a habit-forming brew, a legal intoxicant.

When the build count for the 1970 Boss 302 was finished, it had proven to be a popular version of the Mustang, with 7,013 constructed. So hot was the response from the public, a second plant at Metuchen, New Jersey, was tasked with building the 1970 Boss 302. Another

The second and final year of the Boss 302, 1970's edition was built in significant numbers, with 7,013 units made. The tape stripe was a one-year-only package, standard with the Boss 302. A chin spoiler was fitted to reduce front-end lift at high speed.

factor in the large amount of 1970 Boss 302s built was the SCCA's changing the minimum number of street versions made to qualify for racing. The 1969's need for 1,000 units was raised to 7,000 vehicles for 1970.

In 1970, the SCCA changed the maximum size of the engine to 350 ci, ending the need to build the Boss 302 engine. Other manufacturers competed with larger engines, but lessons learned in

1969 paid off with the Boss 302 Mustang clinching the title in 1970.

Bunkie Knudsen was shown out of the Ford offices in August 1969, but by that time, the 1970 models were starting to be built. His successors would not be as enamored with motorsports as he was; thus Ford started stepping away from competition on the track. That meant the end of the Boss 302 program, a vehicle that existed on the showroom only to

MASSIVE HAMMER, PART TWO

satisfy the needs of racing. The public got the best end of the deal.

Ford had introduced the Boss 429 engine in 1969 in order to satisfy NASCAR's requirement that the engine on the track was based on a street production mill. Its on-track record was a success, as David Pearson took home the trophy as the 1969 Grand National driving champion. Ford enthusiasts prayed for the same sort of result in the 1970 season, but events at the highest levels of the corporation put a fork in that effort. Henry Ford II handed Bunkie Knudsen his walking papers and put Lee Iacocca in his place. Iacocca in turn cut the Ford racing budget by 75%, effectively killing any chance for another NASCAR title. As a result, there was no need to build a minimum number of street 429-ci

Looking like a hungry shark, the 1970 Boss 429 had a menacing presence. Magnum 500 steel wheels were standard on the Boss 429, as were the Goodyear F60x15 tires, the best on the market.

For 1970, the Boss 429 used a black hood scoop, regardless of body color. Incorporating the body changes of the rest of the Mustang line, the big-block racing engine was a very tight fit in the engine compartment, requiring significant modifications of the front shock towers to ease the mill into position.

engines, meaning that the end of the Boss 429 was at hand.

However, the build sequence for the big-block Boss guaranteed that it would be in showrooms for 1970, whether it was needed for homologation purposes or not. Both 1969 and 1970 Boss 429s were built between January and December 1969, with a one-month break in July in order to facilitate retooling for the 1970 models. Because the engine would not enjoy the factory backing on the race track in 1970 that it had the year before,

Ford didn't market the 1970 Boss 429 as heavily as it had the year before. The result was that only 499 units were built, making them even rarer than examples from 1969.

Differences in the Boss 429 from 1969 to 1970 include the adoption of the mildly revised bodywork that spanned the entire Mustang line. That included the elimination of the faux air scoops beneath the quarter windows, à la the 1969 Boss 302. While the huge functional air scoop was body colored on 1969

Boss 429s, it was low gloss black in 1970, regardless of body color. The flat panel between the taillights was painted body color, unlike the blacked-out treatment of 1970 Boss 302s. The more discrete styling in 1970 was offset with the introduction of a number of vivid hues, such as Grabber Blue, Grabber Orange and Calypso Coral. Inside the vehicle, the molded door panels used in 1969 were replaced with conventional armrests mounted on base-level door panels.

The beast under the hood was now only a mechanical-lifter "T" engine. The "S" engine with hydraulic lifters from early 1969 was no longer offered. Performance was the same in 1970 as in 1969. That meant that if a Boss 429 owner didn't want to be embarrassed on the street, the induction and exhaust systems would need to be changed. Still, it wouldn't take long to empty the 20-gallon fuel tank. Power steering was standard, its "Fluidic-Control" an early type of variable-effort, delivering more boost at low speeds, cutting back on assistance as speeds increase. However, the steering wheel still needed 3.74 turns lock-to-lock. The suspension was identical with 1969, except for the rear anti-roll bar location changing from below the axle in 1969 to above it.

With the end of production in December 1969, the Boss 429 departed from the stage with 1,356 units built for the two model years. Without the desire of Bunkie Knudsen to see Ford winning races, it is doubtful the big Boss ever would have seen the light of day. The Boss 429 was far removed from the original Mustang concept for a lightweight, sporty car. It was a sledgehammer on wheels.

TAKING EXCESS TO EXCESS: SHELBY MUSTANGS, 1969 – 1970

When the new Mustang body style was introduced for 1969, the marketing types at Ford felt that the Shelby brand of modified Mustangs should utilize the platform to present a Grand Touring vehicle, different from earlier years when the name Shelby was synonymous with real racing. Rather than walk away from the name, Ford engineers created a

Mustang derivative that found its closest competition was from the same corral, namely the Mach 1. But the two Shelby models, the GT350 and GT500, played in a different part of the pasture.

For reasons shown earlier, by 1969 Shelby production was firmly in Ford's hands, and the vehicles were being built in Michigan. In order to visually differentiate the GTs from the hot Mustangs, it would take more than paint and stripes. Stylists within Ford were now responsible for creating the latest, and what would be

The interior of the 1969 Shelby GT350 was Comfortable (with a capital "C"). Starting with the luxurious Mach 1 treatment, Shelby installed a number of enhancements, such as remote controlled mirrors, a center armrest, and a wooden handle shifter.

1969 SHELBY GT350

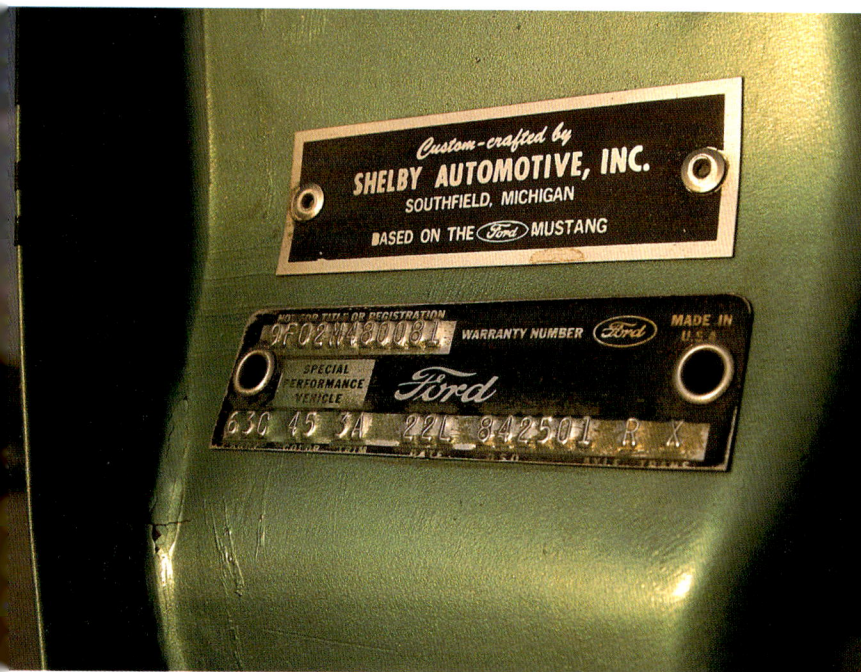

By 1969, GT350/500 production was well in Ford's hands, as suppliers were closer to Michigan than Southern California. These plates were mounted on the driver's door below the latch mechanism.

While Shelby couldn't effect serious changes under the hood, he went to town in the styling department. The long fiberglass hood was matched up to the lengthened front fenders to produce a longer, more dramatic nose. All five NACA vents on the hood were functional. The front pair fed cool air into the engine compartment, while the aft pair vented heated air. Functional ram air went into the center duct, then followed ducting to the air cleaner assembly.

Shelby American worked their magic on the 1969 Mustang, transforming it into the GT350. Equipped with a 351-ci Windsor engine delivering 290 horsepower, the Shelby was a fleet cross-country machine, happiest on the Interstate.

the last, Shelby road car. Using styling cues from the Mustang Milano concept car, they designed a vehicle as large as Carroll Shelby's ambition.

Knockdown vehicles, or Base Vehicle Shells, were pulled from the Dearborn plant, either as a SportsRoof or convertible model. From there the units were sent to Shelby Automotive's plant in Ionia, Michigan. Once there, they were slathered with special body parts, badges, and suspension bits. Being a Shelby, it had to go one better (or bigger) than the regular factory offering, and the GT

models did not deviate. By extending the nose 4 inches, the short deck/long nose proportions were exaggerated. This was done by mounting a lengthened fiberglass hood, replete with five functional NACA ducts to allow air to enter and exit the engine compartment as well as employ ram air. But the front fenders had to be stretched to fit the new body lines. Front fenders made of fiberglass were installed, each side sporting a scoop.

In the finest Shelby tradition, if one scoop is good, nine must be much better. On coupes, large fiberglass scoops were

With a straight stretch of road, or track, the 1969 Shelby GT500 could lift its skirts and hustle with most of the pack. It would get to 60 miles per hour in 6 seconds flat, with the quarter-mile taking 14 seconds at 102 miles per hour, a respectable showing for a 3,850-pound car.

installed under the quarter windows, ironically in the same place the phony scoops were fitted on the Mach 1. But of course, these were larger. On convertible Shelbys, the scoops were lower on the body to a position just in front of the rear wheel wells.

The rear of the vehicle was not ignored either, as a sizeable spoiler was bolted on. As in years past, the broad taillights were sourced from the 1965 Thunderbird. Under the rear bumper were dual, center-mounted aluminum exhaust tips, helping the engines breathe.

Under the long hoods were engines familiar to the Mustang lineup. Customers ordering a $4,434 GT350 got a 351-ci Windsor V-8, topped with a Autolite 470-cfm four-barrel carburetor, rated at 290 horsepower and 385 lb/ft of twist. With the exception of the Shelby using an aluminum intake manifold and finned aluminum Cobra valve covers, it was the same mill used in regular Mustangs which, in fact, was not a bad thing. The Windsor was a relatively light engine, which tended to help handling. All GT350s and 500s were equipped with

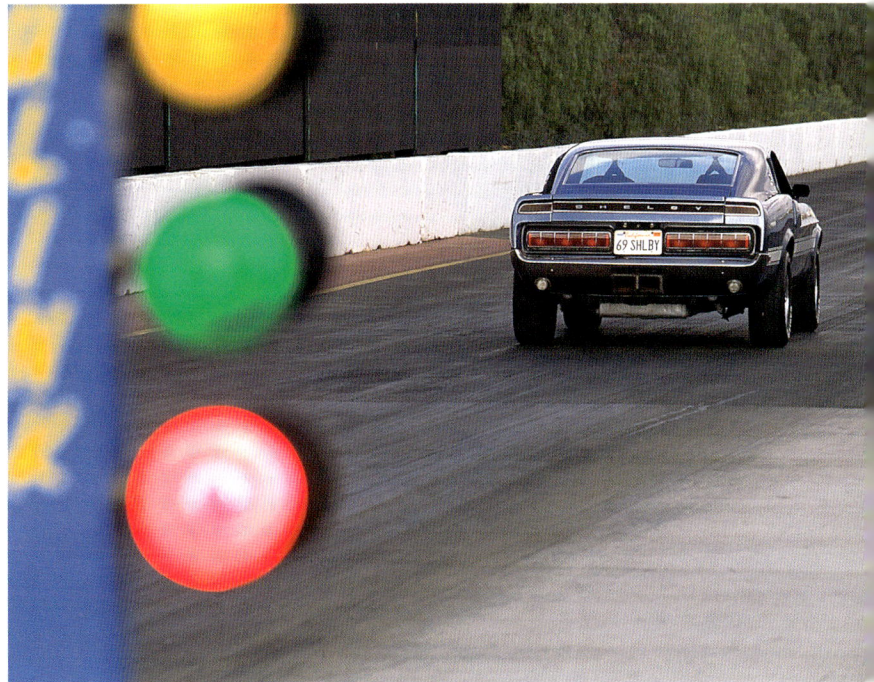

Shoulder harnesses hanging from the roll bar were standard equipment in the 1969 Shelby GT500. In normal street driving, the big-block averaged 11 miles per gallon, but heavy use of the throttle could put consumption in the 9-miles-per-gallon range.

To cover the vents used in the Mustang behind the door handles, Shelby crafted a large scoop to suggest race-ready performance. Taillights were sourced from Ford's 1965 Thunderbird. An alloy exhaust tip was located in the center of the lower valance panel.

the standard Mustang Competition Suspension. In the small-block Shelby, the result was a crisp handling highway cruiser with a $^{55}/_{45}$-weight distribution. Using heavy pressure on the accelerator generated 60 miles per hour on the speedo in the 7.0 to 7.5 second range, commendable for a 3,600-pound road car.

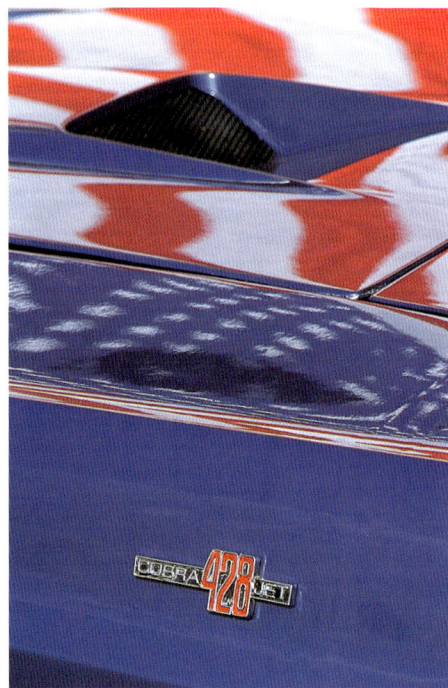

Being a large fiberglass part, the hood tended to bow in time, making for a gap between the fenders and the hood. With a 428 Cobra Jet emblem on the front fender, this must be a 1969 Shelby GT500.

Checking the $4,700 GT500 box on the dealers form resulted in the big 428CJ-R engine getting squeezed between the shock towers. This V-8 delivered 335 horsepower and a beefy 440 lb/ft of torque, enough to get the F60x15 Goodyear Super Wide-Oval tires blurring. In the February 1969 issue of *Sports Car Graphic*, a GT500 was run through its paces, showing that straight-line performance was healthy. In the 0-to-60-miles-per-hour test, the needle swung around in 6.0 seconds, while the quarter-mile was dispatched in 14 seconds at 102 miles per hour. With standard 3.50:1 gears in the differential, top speed came in at 115 miles per hour.

Both models were available with either a 4-speed manual or the Cruise-O-Matic 3-speed automatic transmission. Unlike early Shelby Mustangs, comfort options like air conditioning were on the order sheet. Drivers wanting serious grunt could order the Traction-Lok rear end, but that necessitated leaving out the A/C, so it came down to velocity or comfort. Most buyers opted for the effortless rush of power from the big-block, and the more options the better.

As the 1969 models were rolling onto American roads, Carroll Shelby saw the writing on the wall. The GT350 and 500 were far removed from the lightweight, thinly disguised race cars that Shelby developed in the mid-sixties. He decided that enough was enough and approached Ford vice president John Naughton in late 1969 to ask that the plug be pulled on the Shelby Mustang. Naughton agreed, and the order went out to stop production. By that time, 3,150 were built. Unfortunately, not all of them were sold in model year 1969. To move the remaining 601 cars off dealer lots, they were treated to a pair of hood stripes and a chin spoiler, and the FBI was called in to verify that new serial number plates denoting them as 1970 models were legal. Minor smog equipment modifications were made to ensure the 1970 models fell into line with regulations. When they were gone, the party was over. The Shelby Mustang went out with its head high.

Built in Michigan, the 1969 Shelby GT500 was now a Ford product, with the name of the former racer helping to justify the $4,709 base price. The suspension was the same Competition Package found on the Mach 1, while fiberglass pieces were used to construct the large tail spoiler.

As 789 Shelby GT350/500s went unsold at the end of the 1969 model year, Shelby simply painted on a pair of black hood stripes, changed the VIN tag to read a 1970 build date, and upgraded the emissions package to move the unsold cars. A chin spoiler was added to complete the transformation into 1970 vehicles.

A pair of stripes a 1970 Shelby GT350 makes. These twin stripes and a front chin spoiler were the only visible changes between the 1969 and 1970 models. But the view out the windshield still looked like the flight deck on an aircraft carrier.

The shifter in the 1968 Shelby GT500KR was a no-nonsense affair, an easy-to-grasp lever that welcomed fast behavior.

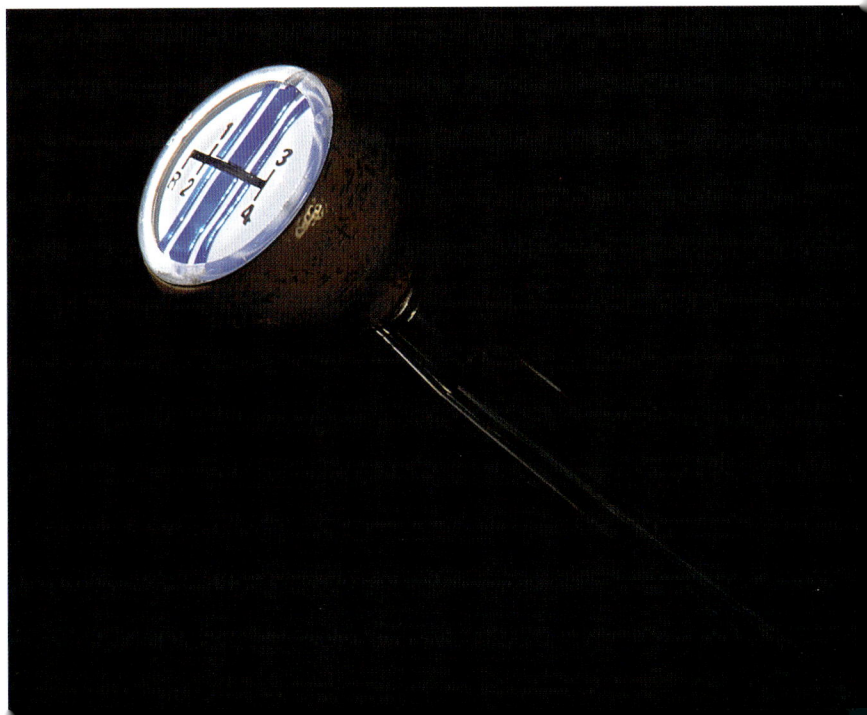

1970 MUSTANG MACH 1

The second year of producing the largest Mustang to date, the Boss 429, turned out to be its last. Ford heard the throngs of buyers clamoring for more power, and the easiest and cheapest way to deliver the grunt was to increase cubic inches. However, getting the engines to fit under the Mustang's long hood was a different matter. Some engines, such as the giant Boss, needed "modifications" to the engine compartment sheet metal, usually with a hammer. To avoid such crude assembly, Ford decreed that the next generation of Mustangs would be able to swallow any and all power plants. This dictated a cavernous engine bay, which meant the rest of the vehicle had to grow. Thus, the 1970 model was the last scene of the act. Front and center in the public eye was the popular Mach 1.

For its second year on the market, the Mach 1 continued to deliver a wide range of power options tailored to every budget.

Buyers searching for a strong Mach 1 in 1970 didn't need to look any farther than one equipped with the 428 Cobra Jet engine. Capable of getting up to 60 miles per hour in only 5.7 seconds, it churned out tremendous torque, 440 lb-ft at 3,400 rpm, and could be driven around town without a complaint.

From a 351-ci V-8 using a 2-barrel carburetor, to a 428-ci Super Cobra Jet monster designed to hurl itself down the drag strip, the Mach 1 hit its stride in public acceptance. Stylistically, the Mach 1 was cleaned up for 1970. Immediately noticeable was the removal of the faux air scoops under the quarter windows. These were replaced with the smooth contours that Larry Shinoda insisted on for the 1969 Boss models. The outboard headlights were replaced with simulated vents,

returning the Mustang to a two-headlight vehicle. At the other end, the concave taillight panel was changed to a flat affair with flush taillights. All Mach 1s used a prominent rocker panel treatment to denote their sporty intentions. A full range of options were still available, such as rear window slats, rear spoiler and Ram-Air induction.

At the heart of any Mach 1 is the engine . . . some for show, some for serious go. Base power for the 1970 Mach 1

Stylistic changes in the 1970 Mach 1 included eliminating the scoops behind the door handles, returning to a two-lamp headlight system, and a rocker panel treatment. The powerful 300-horsepower, 351-ci Cleveland engine debuted in the 1970 Mustang, costing only $48 in the Mach 1 and $93 in other Mustangs.

was the excellent 351-ci Cleveland V-8 topped with a 2-barrel carb. With 250 horsepower, it wasn't about to rip the rubber from the rims, but it didn't require constant maintenance either. Stepping up the ladder, a Mach 1 buyer could pick the same engine, but using a 4-barrel carburetor. This potent small-block was rated at 300 horsepower. Using heads that closely resembled those on the Boss

302, it was a power plant that relished high rpms. For the driver that "needed" yet a bigger hammer, there was an available big-block. With 428 cubic inches, it was advertised as having 335 horsepower. It had that, and plenty more. Those seeking the top of the line could check the Drag Pak option ($155). This had the factory stuffing more go-fast equipment under the hood, such as

427-type connecting rods, an engine oil cooler and a different harmonic balancer. This turned the Cobra Jet into the Super Cobra Jet, meant to dominate on the drag strip.

All Mach 1s could be bought with a Ram-Air shaker hood, and tests seemed to indicate that at high speeds, power was boosted slightly. Visually, few automobiles could hold a candle to a Mach 1. It radi-ated power and speed. Ford created a legend in its own time which would carry the Mustang forward for three more years. So strong is the Mach 1 moniker, Ford re-released a Mustang Mach 1 for 2002. When a manufacturer uses a name 33 years after its debut, it's a genuine hit with a bullet.

The 1970 Mach 1's base engine was this 351-ci Cleveland V-8, equipped with a two-barrel carburetor. Rated at 250 horsepower at 4,600 rpm, it made sufficient power to satisfy the Mach 1 buyers who wanted to look like they could blow someone's doors off even if the engine didn't play the game.

This tape graphic treatment flanking the hood scoop was unique for 1970 Mach 1s, with the engine displacement displayed in cubic inches. Once again, the scoop was there for looks, as it did not ingest air. An optional Shaker hood was available for $65 on the Mach 1.

The diminutive trunk of the 1970 Mach 1 did not encourage a lot of luggage on trips. Adding the rear spoiler to the trunk lid overpowered the strength of the springs holding the trunk open, requiring Ford to fit a prop rod to keep the compartment open.

Fit for cave dwellers, the 1970 Mach 1's rear seating area was ideal for small children and little else. Fortunately, the seat back folded flat, creating a large storage area behind the front seats.

1970 TWISTER SPECIAL

(above) The Kansas City Ford sales district was looking for a promotional Mustang, and Ford had a number of modified vehicles collecting dust after a supplier company went bankrupt. The result was the Twister Special, of which only 96 were built.

(right) The hope was to have the entire run of Twister Specials fitted with 428 SCJ engines, but a shortage of these forced Ford to install a number of 4-barrel 351-ci Cleveland V-8s instead. This is a 428 Super Cobra Jet example, as evidenced by the placement of the oil cooler mounted on the driver's side of the hood latch.

Due to Kansas City's propensity for tornadoes, it was felt that the label for the limited edition Mach 1s should reflect the area's high velocity heritage.

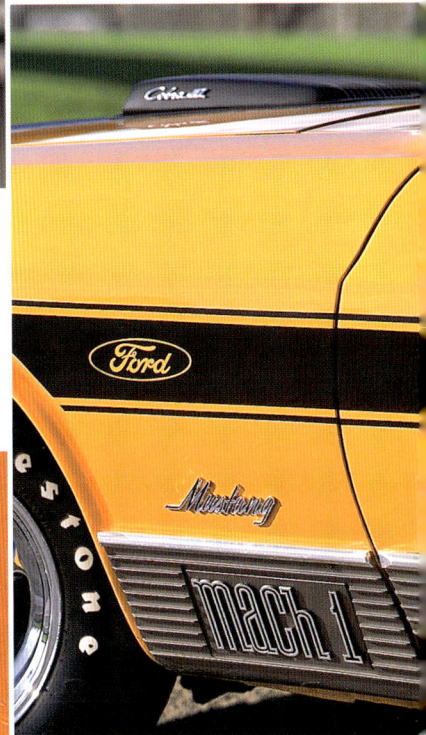

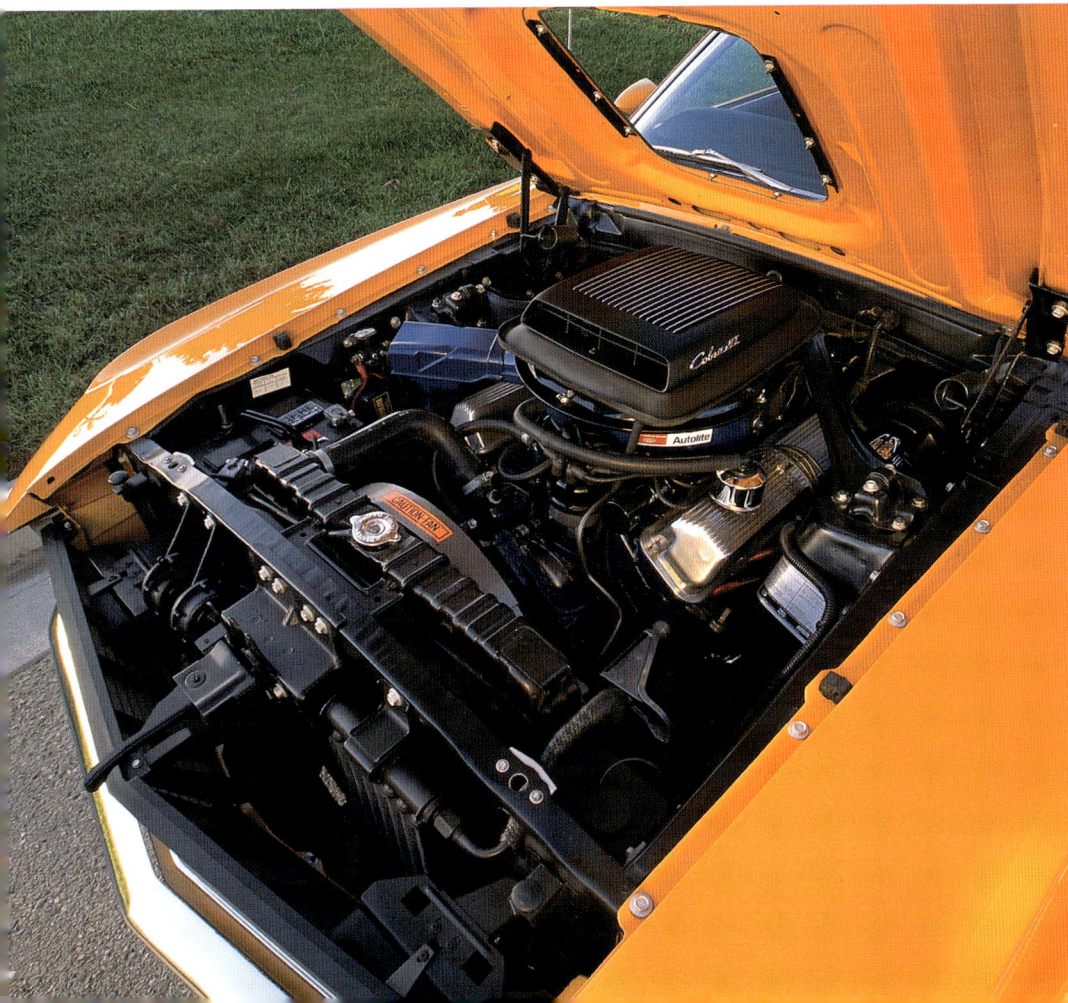

Special striping was used on the 1970 Mustang Twister Specials, eliminating any doubt as to the pedigree of the vehicle. The Cobra Jet Shaker hood scoop wasn't just for effect.

1971–1973

Sales figures for the 1973 Mach 1 were actually good, with 35,440 units sold. With a base price of $3,088, the buyer got a lot of car for the money. But the time had come for the big Mustang to fade into the sunset and make room for its replacement, the Mustang II.

CHAPTER 4
BIGGER IS ... WELL, BIGGER

In the 1960s, Detroit was determined to outdo the competition, whether in power, styling, or flash. The horsepower war was in full flower, with each manufacturer racing to put bigger and faster vehicles into the showroom. For enthusiasts, this was a case of having too many riches. But in case somebody somewhere was having too much fun, storm clouds on the horizon were rolling in from Washington, D.C.. The Clean Air Act, with its amendments courtesy of Senator Muskie, stipulated that car makers start to clean up their act in regards to air pollution. Automotive emission controls were in their infancy, forcing Detroit to dial down engine output to meet regulations. While nobody in Washington decreed that muscle cars were to be banished, the standards that the manufacturers faced meant that the ground-pounders were living on borrowed time.

An adjustable rear spoiler was part of the standard 1971 Boss 351 package, as were the decals similar to the sort used on the Boss 429s of 1969 and 1970. For such a long vehicle, the trunk was diminutive, but the Boss 351 was not meant to carry heavy loads.

1971 BOSS 351

In the spring of 1967, Ford stylists under the supervision of Gene Bordinat started to lay pen to paper to create the Mustang for 1971. Horsepower was selling cars at a frenetic pace at that time, and the suits in Dearborn knew that in order to stay competitive in the muscle car arena, bigger engines would need to slip under the hood. The 1969–1970 era Mustangs had used the huge 428 and 429 engines only after significant modifications had taken place, including cutting and welding of the shock towers. This didn't leave any room for the creature comforts that customers were starting to clamor for, such as power steering, brakes, and air conditioning. With this information, the designers factored in an engine compartment that could hold any engine Ford could dream of building. Bunkie

Knudsen walked into the styling studio on January 18, 1968, and as recounted in Gary Witzenburg's book *Mustang!*, "'He approved the 1971 right in the studio,' recalled Mustang chief designer Gail Halderman. 'We asked if he didn't want to take it outside and look it over, and he said, "No, I like it right here." We said, "Well, there are a couple more being done, wouldn't you prefer to wait and see how they turn out?" He said, "No, I like this one." We had never had approvals like that before.'"

To handle the power plants envisioned by the marketing department, the engineers had to design suspension components that could handle the stress. These added weight which, in turn, required yet beefier parts. By the time the 1971 model was finalized, the Mustang had grown again. The wheelbase was

With its Wünibald Kamm-inspired rear end designed to minimize drag, the 1971 Boss 351 looked bigger than the year before because it was bigger. Track was increased by 3 inches, wheelbase lengthened to 109 inches, and weight was up by 800 pounds. The huge rear window lay at 14 degrees from horizontal.

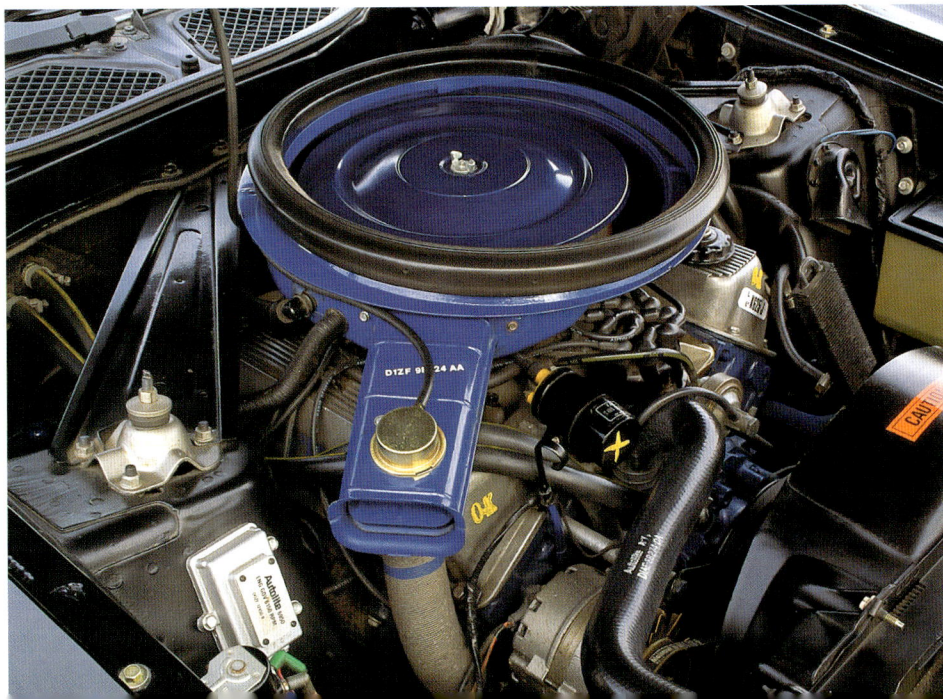

The small silver Autolite box on the rear wheel housing is the rev limiter, meant to keep the engine's internal parts internal. The small heat exchanger in front of the left bank of cylinders is the power-steering cooler, needed for intended Trans-Am racing. While the racing faded from the Boss 351's future, the cooler stayed.

Standard in the 1971 Boss 351 were functional Ram Air hood scoops and locking pins. Two scoops fed a common plenum that sat on top of the air cleaner assembly, feeding cooler ambient air to the engine.

enlarged 1 inch, to 109, while the overall length of the body was stretched 2 inches. With wide engines came the need to expand the body, which grew 2 inches as well. Build a bigger vehicle, and the weight will come, in this case 600 pounds.

Ford had planned on competing in the Trans-Am racing series for 1971; however, the Boss 302 engine was starting to get a bit long in the tooth for a racing car. The answer was already in the Ford inventory, the 351-ci HO Cleveland engine. It cost less than the Boss 302 engine and delivered more power. Rated at 330 horsepower at 5,400 rpm, it was a rugged engine that had proven itself in the 1970 Mach 1. As used in the 1971 Boss 351, the crankshaft was a cast piece holding the bottom end of forged connecting rods. Aluminum forged pistons helped bring the compression ratio up to 11:1, putting the premium fuel to good use. A 750-cfm D1ZF-9510 Autolite carburetor sat on an aluminum dual-plane intake manifold, while dual exhaust pipes ended under the rear bumper. The differential was filled with standard 3.91:1 Traction-Lok gears to

handle rapid gear changes with the Hurst shifter on the 4-speed manual transmission.

Handling bits were pure Mustang, as Boss 351s came with the Competition Suspension. That meant heavy-duty springs and staggered rear shocks, as well as front and rear anti-sway bars. On the road, the Boss 351 showed the years of development to good effect. As *Car and Driver* wrote in their February 1971 issue, "The engineers come off as the real heroes in the development of the Mustang Boss 351. It offers drag strip performance that most super cars with 100 ci more displacement will envy and generates high lateral cornering forces." Power steering on the Boss 351 was the GM variable-ratio setup, and it contributed to improved steering feel. The price for such cornering prowess was a very firm ride. Wheel travel was limited due to the demands of the stylists for a low design. The fastback body style was a full inch lower than the 1970 model, and while it helped the visual proportions of the car, it did nothing for the suspension engineers. Such a low roofline and high rear deck mandated a rear window the

For 1971, the Boss 351 packed the 330-horsepower 351 HO Cleveland small block engine. This mill was essentially a larger Boss 302 engine, including huge valves, solid-lifter cam, and four-bolt main-bearing caps on all five main bearings. A 750-cfm Autolite 4-barrel carb sat atop an aluminum dual-plane intake manifold, helping deliver 370 lb-ft of torque at 4,000 rpm.

The final year of Boss production resulted in the 1971 Boss 351, a car in search of a race series. When Ford pulled out of racing in November 1970, the Boss 351 was already rolling into dealerships. Because of rules changes, Ford had engineered the Boss 351 to take advantage of rules allowing larger displacement power plants. Only 1,806 Boss 351s were built.

size of Kansas, and almost as flat, the glass being only 14 degrees from horizontal. This in turn affected outward visibility. Massive C-pillars and a long hood prevented drivers from seeing anything on the road close to the vehicle. But if the driver catches a glimpse of something in the rear window, pushing the gas pedal will allow the 370 lb-ft of torque to hustle the 3,345-pound pony car down the road.

In March 1971, *Road Test* magazine strapped on a fifth-wheel test rig and found a 0-to-60 time of 5.9 seconds. The quarter-mile was covered in 13.98 seconds at 104 miles per hour. Top speed was limited by the Autolite limiter, keeping engine speed below 6,500 rpm. In fourth gear, that translated to 123 miles per hour.

Only 1,806 1971 Boss 351s were built, as America was getting tired of thirsty road rockets that had limited backseat and trunk room. For the small number of owners though, the Boss was the most refined of the entire line. Unfortunately, Ford decreed that the entire menu of Ford products would be using unleaded fuel for 1972. That would require reducing the compression ratio to the point that power would be a shadow of its former self. Because the Boss line had been a valuable model, the decision was made to kill production at the end of 1971. Thus, the Boss 351 was a single-year pony, a Grand Tourer that could kick up its heels with the best. Ford pulled the Boss off the stage with the crowd wanting more.

1971 MACH 1

Still on the scene, and still offering multiple engines, was the Mach 1 for 1971. For everyday commutes, a 302-ci V-8, as well as the sturdy 351-ci Cleveland was waiting. But for drivers who wanted to make a strong statement, as well as waste a set of rear tires, the engine to order was the famed 429 Cobra Jet Ram Air or 429 Super Cobra Jet Ram Air.

Engine one, the 429 CJ, generated a healthy 370 horsepower at 5,700 rpm. Unlike years past, it was available with air conditioning and an automatic transmission. Costing $372, the Cobra Jet engine was a tractable power plant that would putter around town without a complaint and then press your spine into the high-back seats when called upon. For additional bragging rights, a buyer could pony up $436 for the 429 Cobra Jet-Ram Air option. The CJ-R used dual hood scoops to feed cool air into a plenum on top of the air cleaner. Both options, rated at 370 horsepower, utilized hydraulic valve lifters, four-bolt main bearing caps, and a hefty Quadrajet 700-cfm four-barrel carburetor.

The crew at *Sports Car Graphic* ran a Mach 1 Cobra Jet through its paces in their October 1970 issue, and the specs bear a closer look. Their 0-to-60 time of 6.3 seconds is flat-out quick, while the drag strip was handled in 14.6 seconds at 99.4 miles per hour. Like the Boss 351, a rev limiter kept rpms below 5,800, thus top speed with a 3.50:1 rear end ratio was 125 miles per hour. With 450-lb-ft of torque, it wouldn't take long to reach ticketable speeds.

A Mach 1 stayed in the Mustang line-up for 1971, offered with a 210-horsepower V-8 standard, two 351 Cleveland engines and two 429 powerplants. Ventless side glass was all the rage in Detroit in the late 1960s, the time frame in which the 1971 Mach 1 was penned.

Looking at the performance specs for the Boss 351, the straight-line numbers are not as disparate as the cubic inches might indicate. While the big 429 CJ engine packed a frightening amount of power and torque, it was difficult getting the grunt to the ground. The best tires of the day, Goodyear F70x14 Wide Ovals, simply transformed themselves into molten rubber with a heavy foot on the accelerator. The Boss 351 might not have had the sheer waterfall of torque as the

The gas cap on the 1971 Mach 1 was a pop-open type, but in 1972, a twist type cap was used. This adjustable rear deck spoiler was an option in 1971 and was the same unit used on Boss 351s.

big block, but it could collect rpms at a quicker rate, which translated into competitive times on the track. Mass over the front wheels, in the guise of one heavy hunk of V-8 iron, did nothing for handling, gross oversteer raising its ugly head when a Cobra Jet was pushed into a corner too fast.

The SCJ-R was the ideal tool for moving quickly, a quarter-mile at a time. While it displaced the same number of cubic inches as the "regular" Cobra Jet,

its internals were changed. Mechanical valve lifters replaced the hydraulic units in the CJ, and a 780-cfm Holley carburetor and forged pistons added reliability. Ford listed the power of the SCJ-R at 375 horsepower, an admittedly modest increase for $531 over the price of a base V-8. There were a number of mandatory options as well, such as the Drag Pak option, front disc brakes, and either a 3.91:1 or 4.11:1 rear axle ratio.

Super Cobra Jets came into their own

when owners would uncork the exhaust system and replace the rear tires with sticky rubber. Then the driver simply had to aim the big block Mustang to a distant point on the horizon and launch. Staggering performance, easily repeatable.

When one considers the number of Mustangs sold in model year 1971 (149,678), the 1,865 Cobra Jet and Super Cobra Jet Mach 1s sold received far more press than their numbers would dictate. But they were marvelous halo vehicles for the entire Mustang line. While the vast majority of 1971 Mustang owners were behind the wheel of tamer versions, they could say that their car was the cousin of a beast. There was a little bit of that in every Mustang.

It just looked like the flight deck of an aircraft carrier. The long hood of the 1971 Mach 1 used a contrasting insert to break up the enormous stretch of metal in front of the occupants.

For 1973, the Mach 1 sported different side-stripe treatment with the logo in front of the rear wheels. As in years before, the tape stripe was reflective.

MACH 1—1972 BIG BLOCKS: GOING, GOING, GONE . . .

In time, regulations finally caught up with the Mustang. The need for reducing air pollution had necessitated the widespread implementation of unleaded fuel. Ford was the first of the manufacturers to engineer the entire product line to use the latest gasoline. Unfortunately, the lower octane rating of the fuel, combined with the reduced compression ratios needed to effectively reduce emissions meant that the upward trend in engine power had come to a rapid halt. In fact, for 1972, all the big block engines were deemed unsuitable in the Mustang. Because they sold in relatively small amounts, the time and money needed to

certify them would have been out of proportion to the numbers produced. Besides, the next generation Mustang, the Mustang II, was deep in development. Thus, performance was in the hands of a single model, the Mach 1. Only two engines were offered, both 351-ci V-8s. But while the big block was no longer on the scene, it must be understood that horsepower ratings were now measured in lower SAE net numbers.

The entry-level engine in the 1972 Mach 1 was a two-barrel 302-cubic inch V-8 that generated only 136 net horsepower. Stepping up the performance ladder started with a 351-ci two-barrel carburetor V-8. Power measured in at 177 horsepower. Buyers wanting a touch more

"oomph" would opt for the 351 Cobra Jet mill, the same engine as the two-barrel version but fitted with a four-barrel carb. While 266 horsepower didn't sound anywhere as strong as prior years, it could still propel the Mach 1 at a healthy clip, if not the ferocious rate of yesteryear. Top dog for 1972 was the 351 High Output (HO), essentially the Boss 351 from 1971, carried over in a detuned state. Available in all Mustang models, it cost $783 when installed in the Mach 1, $812 when dropped into the rest of the line. Compression was reduced to 8.8:1, allowing it to run on regular fuel. A milder camshaft was slipped in, helping the engine to survive on the less potent fuel available. Horsepower was rated at 275 at 6,000 rpm, while torque measured in at 286 lb-ft at 3,800 revs. Not a huge number, but the 351 HO gave a good account of itself on the track.

In a March 1972 *Car and Driver* test, the 351 HO Mustang with a 4-speed manual transmission took only 6.6 seconds to reach 60 miles per hour, while the quarter-mile was tackled in 15.1 seconds at 95.6 miles per hour. A 3.91:1 Traction-Lok rear axle ratio contributed to the quick pace, while top speed was recorded at 120 miles per hour. Underpinnings on the 1972 Mach 1 were a page from the old playbook, mainly a "Competition Suspension," F60x15 Goodyear tires mounted on seven-inch-wide wheels, power front disc brakes, and

In 1973, the Mach 1 used a 140-horsepower, 302-ci engine as the base unit. Two optional engines were on the menu, both with 351-ci displacement. The first rung on the performance ladder was the 177-horsepower 351 Cleveland, while the top powerplant was the 266-horsepower 351 Cobra Jet.

Using the same NASA scoops as in prior years, the 1973 Mach 1 was little changed from the preceding years, except for the gradual erosion of power due to mandated emissions regulations. Getting control of NOx emissions required the development of the EGR system, which allowed for a lean mixture without severe drivability problems.

a manual transmission. Production of the 351 HO was in the neighborhood of 1,000 engines, rare enough to ensure collector status. Except for a label on the air cleaner denoting the powerplant as a 351 HO, there were no external indications of the top-of-the-line mill under the massive hood.

Stylistically, the 1972 Mach 1 was little different from the 1971 model. Sure, the pop-open gas cap had been changed to a standard Mustang unit, but except for a few graphic tape changes, there was very little to visually separate the two years. Ford just wasn't going to spend any money freshening a model that it knew would radically change soon. The Mach 1 was like a race car at the end of a quarter-mile run, just coasting along after crossing the finish line. It would take another model year to close this chapter of the high-performance Mustang, but

Ford had seen sales of the Mustang steadily slip for the last couple of years. For model year 1972, total Mustang sales were only 125,093 units. This was not a sales trend that Ford was pleased about. With the 1973 model, the Mustang came to the end of the HiPo road.

MACH 1—1973: RUNNING QUICKLY INTO THE PAST

Buyers looking at the palette of Ford vehicles in 1973 probably would have noticed that the 1973 Maverick occupied the same place in the lineup that the Mustang of 1965 had filled, that of a right-sized, sporty, affordable car, able to be tailored to the customer's needs and wants. The Mustang had grown into a Grand Touring vehicle, fit for huge engines and rapid acceleration. However, while the Mustang was ensconced in the past, the future was running right past it.

It would take another twenty years for technology to reach a point where performance and social responsibility would co-exist in a single vehicle. Until then, performance vehicles faded from the scene like snow in a spring rain.

It was common knowledge within Ford Motor Company that the big Mustang was just marking time until the new model came onto the scene. Changes for 1973 were made up primarily of tape and graphics. In 1973, buyers in search of performance with a pony in the grille had only one choice, the Mach 1, for $3,088. While the standard engine in the sound-breaker was the 302-ci V-8, with 140 horsepower, two optional engines tried to satisfy the need for speed.

The first extra cost powerplant was the rugged 351 Cleveland, generating 177 horsepower. Using a Motorcraft two-barrel carburetor and 8.6:1 compression,

this value-rich engine cost only $40.79. But for those who just had to have the top-shelf model, spending $194 would entice the line workers to install the Q-code 351CJ. With 248 horsepower at 5,400-rpm, it breathed through a Motorcraft 4-barrel carb. It still used four-bolt main bearing caps holding a cast nodular iron crankshaft and magnafluxed con rods. Included in the Mach 1 package with the 351CJ engine were power front disc brakes, competition suspension, and 55-amp alternator. New for 1973 were slotted forged aluminum wheels, a $110.92 option when fitted onto the Mach 1.

While the 351CJ was no longer the fire-breather it had been a couple of years before, it was still an outstanding basis for owners wanting to wrench on their engine. Yet breaking down the option preferences of buyers showed a leaning

Hood pins lent a performance touch to the Mustang, as did the two-tone paint, which cost $34 on non-Mach 1 Mustangs. Only on 2-barrel 351-ci engines did the hood scoops actually direct air under the hood.

New for 1973 were optional forged aluminum wheels, costing $111 on the Mach 1. Due to metallurgic problems, they had a short run on customer cars. Ford attempted to recall the wheels, but some survive to this day.

toward comfort and convenience, as 90.4% on 1973 Mustangs came with automatic transmissions, while 56.2% enjoyed air conditioning. Clearly, the emphasis was not in tire-smoking performance anymore. Yet with Ford's announcement that the 1973 model was to be the last of the "big" Mustangs, sales improved markedly from 1972. For the last year of the first-generation pony car, 134,267 went out the door. Mach 1 sales accounted for 35,440 of those, a significant increase from the year before. Seems

quite a few buyers recognized that they were seeing the last of a long line of performance-orientated Mustangs.

In hindsight, the first-generation 'Stangs are seen as just the opening chapter in the performance story. Current Mustangs easily match the original cars in acceleration, braking, and handling. But the visual presence of the first nine years of Mustang production is unmistakable, and a rich source of inspiration for future High-Performance Mustangs.

High-back bucket seats had been in Mustangs for a number of years, but the Instrumentation Group, a $71 option, included a tachometer, an ammeter, temperature and oil gauge, and a trip odometer. The AM/FM radio was a hefty $191 extra, while the Rim-Blow steering wheel set buyers back $35.

A sleeper in Mustang clothes, this 1973 model is the hot car for the year. Equipped with a 4-barrel 351-ci engine, it was not possible to get Ram Air with the top engine. 1973 was the first year that radial tires were available as an option.

Luxury, 1973 Mustang style. The Tilt-Away steering wheel, a $41 option, was handy for the long-legged buyer, while the $204 Select Shift Cruise-O-Matic automatic transmission made short work of urban driving. Over 90% of all 1973 Mustangs were so equipped. Shoulder harnesses were $15 extra in the Mustang.

Buyers wanting the 266-horsepower engine spent $194, but Ford tried to certify the 4-barrel 351 with the results of the 2-barrel engine. The EPA found out and was less than pleased. Thus, the Ram Air option was not available with the top power plant.

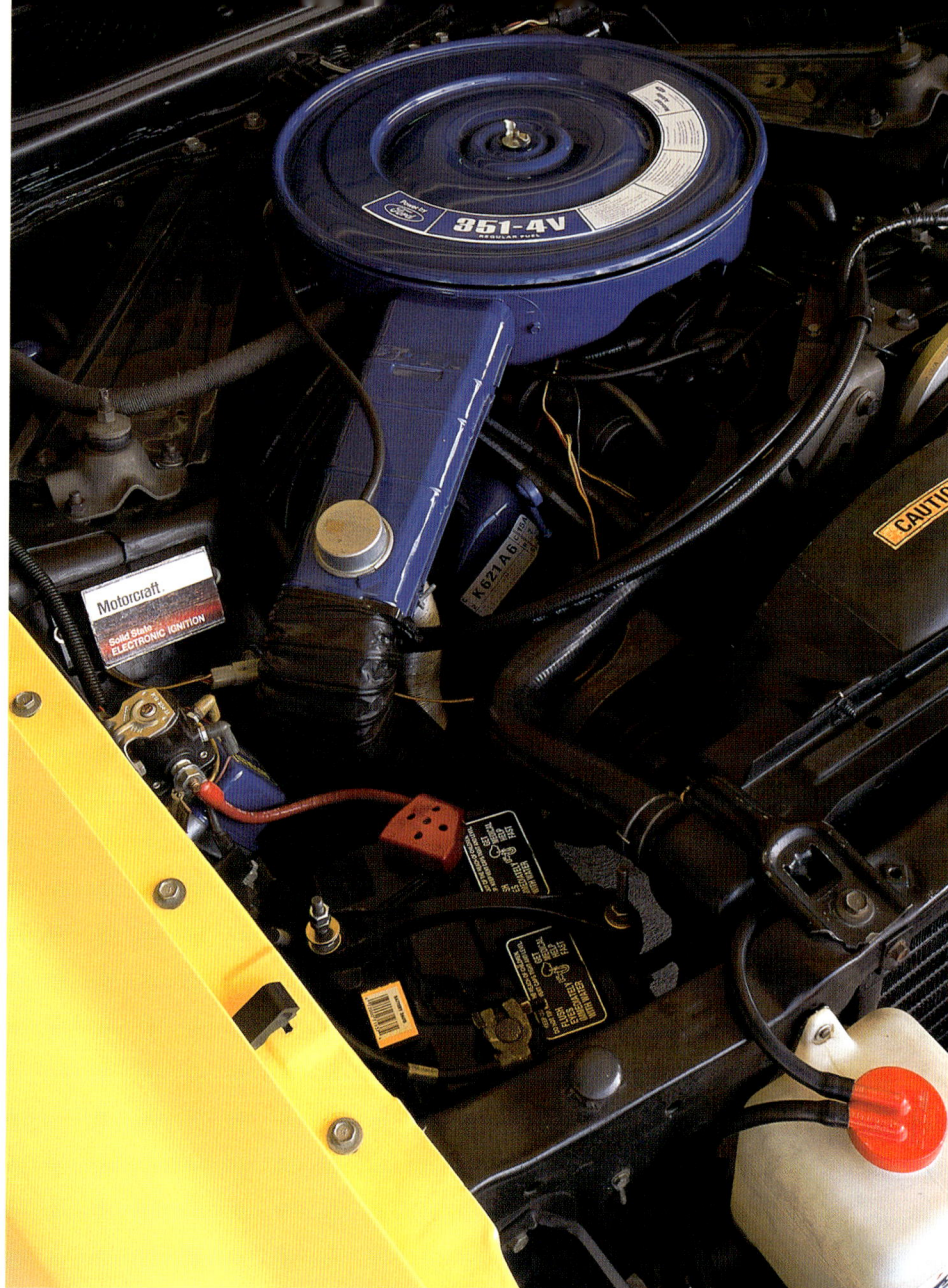

A notchback body style in 1973 was a graceful alternative to the fastback, and the full slate of engines was available. The side stripes, originally made popular on the 1971 Boss 351, were an inexpensive ($31) way to inject visual excitement into the large Mustang.

INDEX

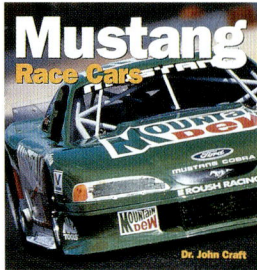

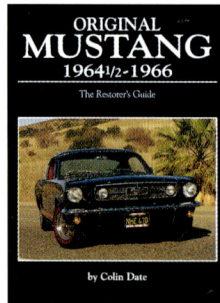

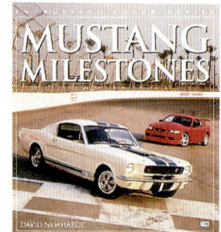

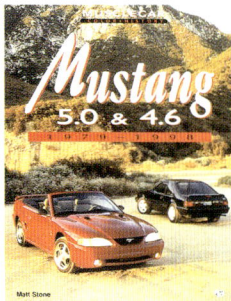

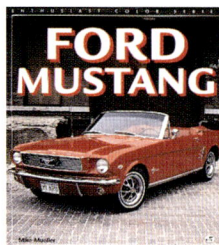

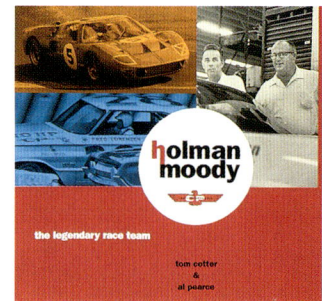

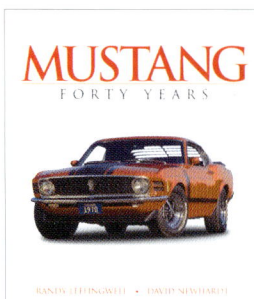

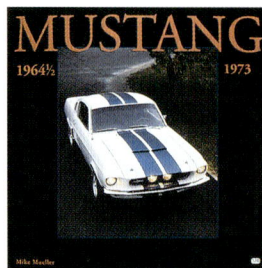

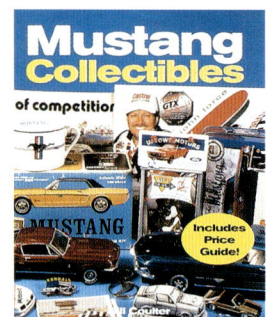